JOURNEY TO COSTUME DESIGN & TECHNICAL THEATRE

College Admissions & Profiles

Rachel A. Winston, Ph.D.

Lizard Publishing is not sponsored by any college. While data was derived by school, state, or nationally published sources, some statistics may be out of date as published sources vary widely based upon the date of submission and currency of numbers. Attempts were made to obtain the best information during the writing of this book from, NCES, U.S. Census Bureau, U.S. Department of Education, Common Data Set, College Board, U.S. News & World Report, college, and organizational sites. Descriptions of colleges are a compilation of college website information as well as student, faculty, and staff interviews with individuals and often from unique experiences and impressions. Attempts were made to triangulate multiple points of light. If you would like to share program information, data, or an impression of a specific college, please write to Lizard Publishing at the address below or at the e-mail address: *info@mylizard.org.*

ISBN 978-1946432520 (hardback); 978-1946432513 (paperback); 978-1946432537 (e-book)

LCCN: 2022901310

Lizard Publishing® 7700 Irvine Center Drive, Suite 800 Irvine, CA 92618 *www.lizard-publishing.com*

Lizard Publishing creates, designs, produces, and distributes books and resources to provide academic, admissions, and career information. Our mental process is fueled by three tenets:

- Ignite the hunger to learn and the passion to make a difference
- Illuminate the expanse of knowledge by sharing cutting edge thinking
- Innovate to create a world that makes the transition from dreams to reality

We work with academic leaders who transform the educational landscape to publish relevant content and advise students of their educational and professional options, with the aim of developing 21st-century learners and leaders. We also work with students to publish their books and present widely diverse ideas to the college/graduate school-bound community. With headquarters in Irvine, California, Lizard Publishing works virtually with authors to edit, publish, and distribute both hard copy and paperback books.

This book was published in the U.S.A. Lizard Publishing is a premium quality provider of educational reference, career guidance, and motivational publications/merchandise for global learners, educators, and stakeholders in education.

Book design by Michelle Tahan *www.michelletahan.com*

Book formatting by Obinna Chinemerem Ozuo

Book website: *www.collegetheatreprograms.com*

LIZARD PUBLISHING

This book is dedicated to Jasmine Jhunjhnuwala, who epitomizes dedication and professionalism.

ACKNOWLEDGMENTS

There is never enough room to acknowledge every person. Numerous people contributed to my perspective about costume design and technical theatre. Students, faculty, counselors, and researchers assisted in enhancing my knowledge base or taught me indelible lessons. Over a lifetime of experiences working with students, I am wiser and more worldly.

I gratefully acknowledge Michelle Tahan, Jasmine Jhunjhnuwala, E. Liz Kim, and Jacqueline Xu, as well as my family, friends, colleagues, and professors. It is with profound gratitude that I acknowledge those I have known in the theatre world.

As a faculty member in the UCLA College Counseling Certificate Program, I met many dedicated counselors who spend their life serving and supporting students. Meaningful contributions to the book have been made indirectly by admissions representatives, college counselors, faculty members who took a special interest in this book's success.

I would also like to thank the thousands of students I have taught, counseled, or supported in my nearly four decades of service.

"If I see so far, it is because I stand on the shoulders of giants."
– Isaac Newton

Isaac Newton once said, "If I see so far, it is because I stand on the shoulders of giants."

A few of those giants whose broad shoulders lifted me higher and helped teach invaluable lessons include: Cheryl Tobin, Sidney Inouye, Corina Lee, Kate Thomas, Matt Bozorgi, Donia Olia, Catharine Malzahn, Anastasia Georgiou, Cammie Clark, Chenoa Craver, Lola Knicker, Lauren Shapiro, Ashley Wayne, Zixuan Lin, Batzi Heger, David Thomas, and Evan Forster.

Finally, there would be no book on costume design and technical theatre schools and no career college admissions counseling without the support of Robert Helmer, whose tireless efforts support me every single day.

ABOUT THE AUTHOR

D r. Rachel A. Winston is a tireless student advocate. She has served the educational community as a university professor, college advisor, statistician, researcher, author, cryptanalyst, motivational speaker, publishing executive, and lifelong student. As one of the leading experts in college counseling and an award-winning faculty member, Dr. Winston has spent her lifetime learning, teaching, mentoring, and coaching students. Her counseling practice centers around college admissions, college essays, portfolios, and intellectual conversations about life and career pursuits.

She started college at thirteen and graduated from college programs in such widely ranging disciplines as chemistry, mathematics, computers, liberal arts, international relations, negotiation, conflict resolution, peacebuilding, business administration, higher education leadership, interpreting, college counseling, and publishing. Throughout her education, she attended and graduated from Harvard, University of Chicago, GWU, UCLA, Syracuse, CSUF, CSUDH, Pepperdine, Claremont Graduate University, University of Texas, and Gallaudet University.

Her position working in Washington, D.C. on Capitol Hill and with the White House in the 1980s took her to approximately a hundred universities training campaign managers at colleges from Colorado to California, thoroughly dotting the western states. Later, she led college tours with students and their families on road trips throughout the United States. She has taught or counseled thousands of students over her career and speaks at conferences and academic programs throughout the world.

As a professor and avid writer for numerous publications, she won the 2012 McFarland Literary Achievement Award, Bletchley Park Cryptanalyst Award, and numerous other awards, including Faculty Member of the Year, Leadership Tomorrow Leader of the Year, and college service and leadership awards. While studying Human Capital at Claremont Graduate University, she was a scholarship recipient at the Drucker School of Management. She was also elected to the statewide Board of Governors for the Faculty Association for California Community Colleges, where she served on their executive committee.

She served as a faculty member for the UCLA College Counselor Certificate Program, the Director of Mathematics at Brandman University, and Embry Riddle Aeronautical University, Chapman University, Cal State Fullerton, and a handful of California Community Colleges, including Cerro Coso College where she also served as the Academic Senate President and retired in 2016. Over her career, she taught mathematics online, on television, live interactive satellite, telecourses, and in large and small lecture halls.

AUTHOR'S NOTE

You are reading this book because you are considering admission to colleges where you open the doors to the world of theatre. Whatever route you took to get to this point, you are in the right place. Right now, you need to gather information to make informed decisions.

While many people offer advice, suggestions differ. Friends will tell you the "right" way or the way their neighbor was accepted. Graciously accept this anecdotal information while you commit to learning more. This opportunity to pursue costume design and technical theatre is available so you can pursue your future.

Dig deeper to consider both expert and current information from counselors who have worked with hundreds of students. Changes in programs, curricula, requirements, and links happen each year.

Double check each program's specifics yourself. This guide is current as of January 2022, with each school's profile information. However, since researching this book, changes may have taken place. There are other books about theatre programs written by talented and experienced counselors. We admire and cheer on their efforts.

> *"We are what we think. All that we are arises with our thoughts. With our thoughts, we make the world."*
> *— Buddha*

This information about colleges, admissions, profiles, and lists is different in that it also provides unique tidbits. We hope you find this information valuable. Your job is to begin early by assembling information for the schools you are considering. Create a road map and set yourself on a clear path.

If you see an error in this book or even a suggestion for a future edition, please write to Dr. Rachel A. Winston at collegeguide@yahoo.com. We will fix the entry with the next printed version. All of that said, this book was written with you in mind.

There is a wealth of information on the Internet with free downloads, FAQs, testimonials, and offers to help you with your applications. Some of these advisors are knowledgeable and can help you. Students and parents hunt around the web, searching for a tremendous number of hours to seek the information they need. We aim to resolve this problem.

This book with college admissions data and profiles was designed to make your search easier. For now, though, we will assume you want to attend school for costume design or technical theatre and are exploring this avenue as a possible way to take advantage of a program to get you on your way toward your goal.

We assume that you are a talented candidate who is willing to work very hard. You may be fascinated with fashion, theatre, or films. Serving others selflessly is virtually a prerequisite for costume design and technical theatre programs.

As you investigate colleges, you might find that some programs are listed in different college departments. Either way, this book will help you reach your goal. Applying to and writing essays for each application will require research to determine which is right for you.

While you might believe that costume design and technical theatre programs are relatively similar, each program's nuances make them very different. These small differences may seem confusing. My goal with this book is to demystify the information and process.

CONTENTS

FOR THE LOVE OF THEATRE: CREATING MAGICAL MOMENTS FOR PATRONS OF THE DRAMATIC ARTS

"An actor and a [theatre] director are both what I would call interpreters of work. We interpret a work, just as a musician will interpret a composer's work; we interpret the work of a playwright. We are servants of the theatre, and I've always believed that. We must serve what has been written; that's what we're there for."

– **George Ogilvie**

A theatre, hushed just before the curtains open, is magical. Patrons who sense that magnificent enchantment, discover a transformative, goosebump-eliciting experience, reminding them that anything is possible. Even a river can be turned into chocolate as Willy Wonka and Charlie Bucket discovered in their search for inner peace and happiness in *Charlie and the Chocolate Factory*. Similarly, Dorothy took a yellow-brick road to discover new friends and braved a menacing forest filled with winged monkeys to discover that her family loved her dearly in *The Wizard of Oz*.

Stories transform concepts and imaginings to writing and from scripts to dramatic re-enactment. Those who eat the cake in *Alice in Wonderland* grow to new heights drinking in the magnificence of the theatre. Simply standing on a pitch-black stage with rows upon rows of empty chairs is a remarkable experience. The stage is a metaphor for life as everyone lives on a stage, performing in their own play. It's humbling.

Shakespeare provided his own commentary.

> "All the world's a stage,
> and all the men and women merely players:
> they have their exits and their entrances;
> and one man in his time plays many parts ..."

—*As You Like It,* Act II, Scene 7, 139–142

Behind the curtain, a different kind of magic happens. Sets create mood and ambiance, depicting grand moments like the balcony scene in *Romeo and Juliet* depicting societal barriers that can thwart love. The riverboat, *Cotton Blossom*, in Jerome Kern and Oscar Hammerstein's musical comedy *Show Boat*, provides a floating palace addressing the social issues of racism and inequality. Each scene transforms into a physical object with the vision, grit, and carpentry skills of technical theatre experts.

Iconic sets like the chandelier in *Phantom of the Opera*, dramatic moments like the helicopter scene in *Miss Saigon*, and a carnivorous, and human-eating plant in *Little Shop of Horrors* bring theatre to spectacular glory. Audience members experience the dynamic sight and sound display.

Meanwhile, Superman dons his cape, Wonder Woman dons an indelible red, white, and blue outfit, accessorized with a gold belt, and Dorothy dazzles the Munchkins with her spectacular ruby red slippers. Identifiable masks like the iconic masterpiece designed by Maria Björnson and worn by the Phantom in *Phantom of the Opera* or the outfits designed by Paul Tazewell and showcased by the *Hamilton* cast stand out in our memories.

As you pursue your goal to become a costume designer or do behind-the scenes work in technical theatre, you will enjoy an exciting career. Have fun using your creative talents, and live each moment fully, developing invaluable skills that are transferable to other jobs you might choose. As you transition, remember that life is a journey, not a destination. Theatre is a thrill ride of grand proportions.

Knowing how to sew and design could lead you into fashion should you decide to change your career. If you can create sets and have carpentry skills, you can build creative spaces in a home or office. Even Halloween sets and costumes can be remarkably fun to produce.

To work in theatre or film, you will find that most professionals with full-time positions have Bachelor of Fine Arts (BFA) or Master of Fine Arts (MFA) degrees in theatre arts. You can earn this degree focused specifically on costume design or technical theatre or a more general degree in theatre arts. Either way, you are set with the general skills. Before, during, and after your educational foundation, you just need experience.

The journey you are taking will have its ups and downs, but you will have stories to tell for the rest of your life. Enjoy this magical experience.

CHAPTER 2

CREATIVITY ON THE SET: ENVISIONING AND CREATING SCENES IN COSTUMES AND SETS

"Great theatre is about challenging how we think and encouraging us to fantasize about a world we aspire to."

– Willem Dafoe

D esign is pure creativity, right? Not exactly. Certainly, ingenuity and innovative idea generation are a must. However, when it comes to theatre, considerably more goes into the thinking process. Costume and set designers must thoroughly conceptualize and internalize the story's big picture. Ultimately, they must envision and execute how they would tell the tale in pictures.

Seven Cs of Costume and Set Design
1. Creative
2. Clear
3. Concise
4. Compact
5. Communication
6. Collaboration
7. Complete

Creativity is fundamental. Afterward, the story's visual imagery needs to be told clearly so that people can see the story and internalize the mood, meaning, purpose, time period, socioeconomic climate, and emotion. The elements of a story are folded into one or more sets of visual pieces – moving parts in a jigsaw puzzle that, alone, says little, but together illuminates the entire picture.

At the same time, the show is not long. The limited timeframe necessitates brevity and conciseness. While plays, musicals, films, and commercials can range in duration, each has a beginning, middle, and end. Each must complete the entire thought with all components fitting together.

The stage or scene is compact in space. All of the action needs to happen within the frame of the stage or a lens. Yet, these components are limited to spatial limitations within the given area. While stages range in size, film locations can be much larger. Nevertheless, there are still bounds on action scenes that can take place on set. Every required image or set piece needed to tell the story must be within the borders.

Shows do not take place in a vacuum. They are visualized and constructed as a team. Not only must the costume and set designers know the story and understand the context, but they must also communicate effectively with the director at the start. From the very beginning, there should be a clear line of communication.

Collaboration is essential. The designer may propose a couple of ideas, though they must be conceptualized with the director's leadership. Consultation with other cast and crew members is also necessary, including the technical director, production manager, scenic charge artist, prop master, costume designers, and other team leaders. By talking through opportunities for improvement, pitfalls in design elements, and financial and spatial limitations, the team can efficiently and effectively produce the synergy to craft the best representation of the story.

In the end, the story must be complete. Whatever needs to be communicated must have its rise and fall. The costumes and sets must reflect the perspective, conflict, climax, resolution, and overall theme.

CHAPTER 3

TECHNICAL SKILLS: SEWING, GRAPHIC DESIGN, MAKEUP, AND SET CONSTRUCTION

"Clothes make a statement. Costumes tell a story."

- Mason Cooley

Theatres are alive, buzzing with activity. Although some might suggest otherwise with the pandemic's challenges, films continued to be created and theatres returned. Omicron's December 2021 heartbreaking shutdown disappointed thousands, though the song "No Day But Today", in the musical *Rent* reminds us,

There's only us,
There's only this,
forget regret,
or life is yours to miss.
No other road,
no other way,
No day but today.

Historically, theatres have always bounced back, even in the most catastrophic times. Shows and styles may change; budgets may tighten; designs may reflect the momentary mood.

While few alive today will ever forget the impact the pandemic had on life, liberty, and disparity, people will remember that "somewhere over the rainbow, bluebirds fly." We, too, will fly again, as will theatre. Unfortunately, the saddest moments will not completely disappear.

Theatres took a huge hit, stopping production teams. Theatre will come back stronger as will those who brought energy and life to the stage. Costumes will be created and stitchers will resume their roles. Feverish tech crews will construct sets, create props, paint miniature villages, and move tons of material.

The song "seize the Day" from the musical Newsies tells us,
Now is the time to seize the day
They're gonna see there's hell to pay
Nothing can break us
No one can make us quit before we're done
One for all and all for one!

SEWING, FABRIC, AND PATTERN MAKING

While creative thinking is at the heart of costume design, sewing is an essential skill. Not all designers know how to sew, but costume designers must. Having these skills before entering college is incredibly valuable—almost a necessity. However, quick learners who put the time into becoming technically accurate and proficient at sewing will do fine provided all of the other design skills are solid.

In addition to using sewing machines and being comfortable with needle and thread stitching, costume design students should be fluent in the various types of fabric. Naming fabric types and having a sense of types of threads and textiles is essential. Play with each type of fabric. Test out stitching, flexibility, and durability. Some fabrics rip while others are so delicate that they run, pull, or cannot be easily used for costumes. Try decorating elements - some work, some fall off.

Part of your college education will be devoted to practice, assessment, and experience. Read what other people have written about their experience with fabrics. Some work and some do not. Learn from others. Experience is a tough teacher, but one that is invaluable as you progress.

Pattern making is a key component, requiring arithmetic and geometry skills. Experiment with fabric, pick up a dozen patterns, and attempt to make the items for yourself. See what works and what does not. Determine the techniques that would improve the pattern and the instructions. Instructions must be clear, so writing and accurate communication skills are a must.

SKETCHING AND GRAPHIC DESIGN

Sketching and graphic design are valuable skills for your long-term career pursuits. Draw out what you see in your mind. Take lessons to improve your drawing skills. Other people need to see what you envision.

Portfolios for costume, set design, and technical theatre admissions may require sketches. Many do not, but some will. Conceptualizing and drawing your ideas on paper is an essential skill. Sketching costume design ideas and sets allows everyone on board to visualize the final outcome. Pattern making also requires drawing and graphic design skills.

You are likely to use digital design software during college like Adobe Creative Cloud (Photoshop, Illustrator, InDesign, Premiere Pro, Acrobat, etc.), AutoCAD, 3DS Max, Revit, or Sketchup. Others may be required at your school. Nevertheless, it is extremely helpful to have graphic design and digital software skills before entering college. Training before and during college is valuable in the long run, probably more so with technology integration into every aspect of our lives.

MAKEUP

While makeup design may not be taught in a college class, it is an indispensable component of an actor's on-stage appearance. The technical details of makeup artistry are significantly more complicated than makeup you might purchase for everyday wear.

First, the makeup applied to the face and body needs to last through complex scenes that require dancing or excessive movement. Second, how makeup is applied and the designs created can be thoroughly artful. Third, applying makeup for theatre and film is not the same as for daily wear. Finally, while developing skills in character makeup, special effects, and emergency medical visuals, you may also need to create realistic, contemporary looks for the stage and film.

Good makeup artists are paid very well. If you are not taught makeup design in your college classes, you should take master classes in makeup artistry.

CONSTRUCTION AND CARPENTRY

While most people realize that technical theatre involves the building and movement of sets, construction and carpentry can add additional problem-solving challenges. There are a myriad of details to consider. One error could send someone to an emergency room or ruin an entire show. Sets must be sturdy and safe but light enough and moveable. Nails cannot stick out and wheels need to be greased and working properly. Wood must be sanded and painted in such a way that splinters do not puncture the hand of someone on the crew or an actor. Materials need to be used that do not catch on a garment. Fire retardants, paints, gels, and coatings may be used as well. Chemicals must be non-toxic since the unexpected may eventually happen.

Numerous job postings for technical theatre jobs list lifting heavy materials as a requirement. There are good reasons why. The material used in many sets can weigh significant amounts. People in technical theatre often have multiple roles but one of them is to lift boxes that need to be transported from one location to another. Boards, metal rods, and casters can be heavy. Strength is essential to lift sets and set components. Weightlifting may not seem like an essential skill, but do not be surprised.

The keys to success are to know yourself and develop skills. Whether you pursue costume design or set construction, you are likely to assume roles and be required to perform tasks outside of your area of expertise. The motto of the Boy Scouts and Girls Scouts is to "Be Prepared." That concept fits especially well behind the scenes of a theatre.

CHAPTER 4

ACADEMIC SKILLS: FOUNDATIONAL ACADEMICS FOR TELEVISION, PLAYS, AND MUSICALS

"I grew up backstage and on movie sets, and I thought they were the most magical places on Earth."

– Zosia Mamet

Knowing history, politics, sociology, economics, and literature is extremely important to be skilled in all aspects of theatre. These essential ingredients, along with significant historical and sophisticated research, allow you to unfold the story with clarity.

DRAMATURGY

Plays, films, and musicals exist in a context. While actors act, singers sing, writers write, and directors direct, a dramaturg gives meaning. While a dramaturg bridges directors and actors, they also construct the meaning of the plays, films, or musicals. You do not need to be a dramaturg, but it is important to know as much as possible about the elements of each show or story.

Dramaturgy encompasses the fundamental principles of drama that explore and represent the context of a play, film, or musical. A dramaturg adapts a work for the stage.

Think of dramaturgy as a way to lay a foundation and build a structure for a theatrical show so that the director can formulate the concept, the actors can translate the message, the costume designers can provide the style, and the technical theatre director can construct a meaningful set that fits the context of the performance.

An interpretive analysis of all aspects of the performance forces the director and often key players to engage in critical thinking regarding the show's narration as well as develop the foundational aesthetic underpinnings. Thus, dramaturgy offers a comprehensive exploration into the storyline, scene, and society to provide a compelling context for the viewer. For example, setting the stage for the audience so that they can conceptualize the totality of the theatrical performance is essential.

Dramaturgs must love to read, interpret, write, and ask questions. They also must check facts. Plays and films are cancelled because they are incorrect. Social media outpourings denouncing inaccurate scenes, speeches, or portrayals can stop shows in production. Thus, dramaturgs must consider history and culture carefully to clarify, adapt, and bring stories to life.

Knowledge of dramaturgy helps to translate to the audience the historical elements of the story, contemporary understanding of the topic, and the importance of sharing the lessons to be learned. From the word choices and memorable quotes to emotion and expression, knowledge of dramaturgy is a valuable component of a theatre arts degree.

Famous dramaturgs include:

- Caryl Churchill: British playwright
- Peter Davis: American theatre historian, actor, director, and educator
- Gotthold Ephraim Lessing: German writer, philosopher, and dramatist
- Kristína Farkašová: Slovak actress, singer, comedienne, editor, and blogger
- Kentarō Kobayashi: Japanese comedian, actor, and theatre director
- Gideon Lester: American artistic director and creative art producer
- Julie McIsaac: Canadian stage director, playwright, and creator
- Heiner Müller: German dramatist, poem writer, and theatre director

ANALYSIS, CLARITY, AND ORGANIZATION

Efficiencies in spatial design are also essential. The stage is compact. Too many costume and set changes make the show cumbersome for the crew. Thus, how can the story be told in the most robust, exciting, and dynamic way with the least amount of external effort?

Designers read and analyze. They must clarify and organize information. By sifting through the story they can latch onto visual cues and conceptual approaches that most clearly support the ideas depicted, value orientation, and overall theme. Open-mindedness begins with perspective and a wide view of what is happening in the world, discovering intrigue in the mundane of life, as well as what is happening during the designated time period.

From sadness and agony to humor and exultation, emotion is not only brought out through the script and acting, but in all areas of the theatre. Humans are visual creatures. They will see first and process the lines spoken by the actor second. Costume designers and technical theatre directors must learn how people feel, what they love, and what makes them afraid. Mood can be set with ominous trees, a weathered barn, scarecrows in a cornfield, a rusted sewer, blissful ocean waves, or starry nights.

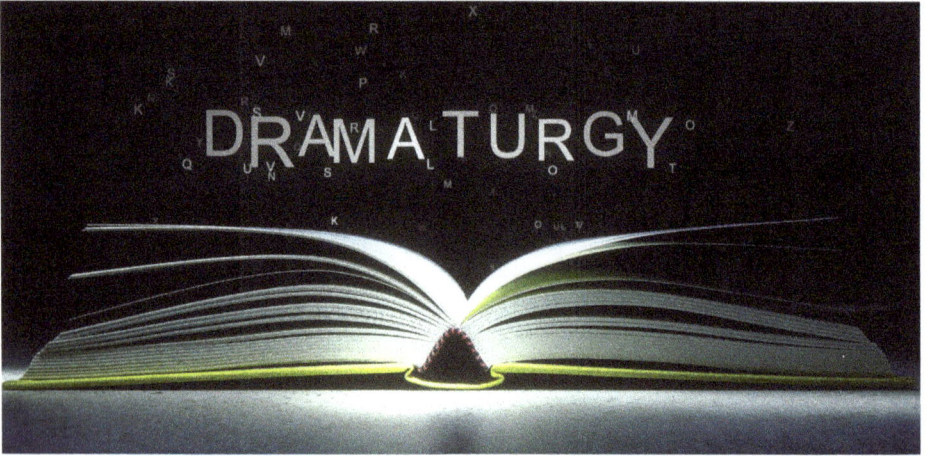

THE IMPORTANCE OF LIBERAL ARTS

You can attend college to be trained in a skill or you can get an education that will last a lifetime across disciplines. Think of this type of approach to learning like the proverb, "If you give a man a fish, he eats for a day; If you teach a man to fish, he eats for a lifetime." The liberal arts is a holistic approach to education, offering you limitless possibilities to learn in areas you never would have chosen but shift your thinking so profoundly that you view life with a newfound approach.

By reading across disciplines, a broader view of scenes and ideas can be formulated and curiosity generated. Thus, knowledge gained in college can turn the wheels of creativity. Classes in art, architecture, and culture add context and ambiance. Imagine a new world, build it, and invite the audience to enter.

The pursuit of knowledge and the process of inquiry are both powerful, building upon ancient philosophy and the universal desire to understand what is commonly not known. Thus, by asking questions, critically analyzing arguments, solving problems, reading literature, understanding political viewpoints, learning geography, and delving into philosophy you develop skills that traverse whatever career you pursue. According to the World Economic Forum's Report, *The Future of Jobs and Skills*,[1]

In many industries and countries, the most in-demand occupations or specialties did not exist 10 or even five years ago, and the pace of change is set to accelerate. By one popular estimate, 65% of children entering primary school today will ultimately end up working in completely new job types that don't yet exist.1 In such a rapidly evolving employment landscape, the ability to anticipate and prepare for future skills.

In a rapidly changing job market with the infusion of technology, changes in organizational behavior, and focus on outcomes-based processes, interdisciplinary cross-training is a necessity. If you aspire to lead an organization or manage a project, you will need diverse knowledge in the humanities and social sciences along with strong skills in digital marketing and digital design. Be hungry to learn. Broaden your worldview with an open-minded approach, values-centered mindset, and the passionate quest to dig deeper into ideas.

Due to the disruptive changes in society, the landscape of schools and careers will change. Drivers of social change including globalization, digital currencies, and shifts in communication have accelerated and will significantly impact jobs. Those with the most versatile skills will thrive. Thus, a liberal arts education is even more important than ever. So, take advantage of whatever you can learn today.

Carpe Diem – "Seize the Day!"

---

1   World Economic Forum, "Chapter 1: The Future of Jobs and Skills," *World Economic Forum*, n.d., http://reports. weforum.org/future-of-jobs-2016/chapter-1-the-future-of-jobs-and-skills/

CHAPTER 5

GAINING EXPERIENCE: INTERNSHIPS FOR HIGH SCHOOL, COLLEGE, AND BEYOND

"If you are not willing to learn, no one can help you. If you are determined to learn, no one can stop you."

– Zig Ziglar

ACKNOWLEDGMENT OF THE PANDEMIC'S IMPACT ON THEATRE

To begin, the pandemic's impact on theatre cannot go unnoticed. Theatres around the world were impacted by COVID-19 and its numerous repercussions. Theatres were shuttered. Though many that could survive the financial impact reopened, casts, crew, and directors needed to find alternative opportunities, retrain, or use their skills in creative ways. Internships were difficult to find for students who counted on gaining experience. Many school plays and musicals were canceled. However, new opportunities opened. Schools resumed shows and theatre programs from high school to graduate school.

INTERNSHIP LOCATIONS

Some geographical locations lend themselves better to internships for costume design and technical theatre. Larger cities where there are big stages or where the region's donors support theatre offer more chances to gain internship experiences. However, colleges with costume design and technical theatre also provide their students with internal opportunities to gain experience.

For example, New York City offers the greatest diversity of theatre internship options. In addition, nearby areas in New Jersey, Connecticut, Long Island, and Westchester Counties also offer significant opportunities for internship experience and professional positions. Some colleges in the New York and New England areas have a close affiliation with major theatres. For example, the University of Connecticut is connected to the Metropolitan Opera Hartford Stage and offers study abroad opportunities with Bournemouth University College of the Arts and London University Wimbledon College of the Arts in the United Kingdom.

London is a mecca for theatre. An internship or semester abroad at a school, training in costume design and technical theatre is a phenomenal opportunity. Though the theatre community suffered during the pandemic, London theatre will rebound with the robust support of patrons of the arts.

Other locations where there are significant opportunities for theatre include:

Atlanta	Miami/Ft. Lauderdale
Austin	Minneapolis/St. Paul
Boston	Philadelphia
Chicago	Phoenix
Cleveland	Portland
Dallas/Ft. Worth	San Diego
Hartford	San Francisco/Oakland/Berkeley
Los Angeles/Orange County	Washington, D.C./Maryland/Virginia

ArtsAmerica also explains, "But even some cities and towns that don't have an especially large or active year-round theatre scene are noteworthy for festivals and other events; one famous example is Louisville, Kentucky, where the Actors Theatre of Louisville hosts the annual Humana Festival of New American Plays."[1]

Look through TheatreWorksUSA for some of the many opportunities available: *https://twusa.org/about/work-with-us/*

SUMMER TRAINING & INTERNSHIPS – MIDDLE SCHOOL & HIGH SCHOOL

In theatre, students learn by doing. Thus, initial and necessary experiences are often in school and community-based theater programs. Some of the following internships are for acting, musical theatre, technical theatre, and backstage opportunities. However, there are numerous summer options for students to pursue their dream and hone their craft. The following are a few of the summer options.

- ArtsBridge Summer Drama Programs
- AMDA (American Musical and Dramatic Academy) High School Summer Conservatory (Los Angeles and New York)

---

1   Arts America, "Theater," *Arts America,* n.d., http://artsamerica.org/genres/genres-theater/

- Boston Conservatory
- Broadway Artists Alliance Summer Intensives
- BroadwayEvolved NYC Summer Intensive
- Carnegie Mellon University, Pre-College Drama
- Emerson College
- Florida State University
- French Woods Festival of the Performing Arts
- Idyllwild Arts Teens & Kids Summer Program
- Interlochen Arts Camp
- Ithaca College Summer Theatre Intensive
- La Jolla Playhouse Conservatory
- Marymount Manhattan
- Muny/Webster Intensive – St. Louis, Missouri
- Neighborhood Playhouse, Six Week Summer Acting Intensive
- Northwestern University, National High School Institute (Cherubs)
- NYU, Tisch, Summer High School
- Oklahoma City University
- Paper Mill Playhouse, Summer Musical Theater Conservatory
- Penn State University
- The Performing Arts Project (TPAP) – Wake Forest University
- Perry-Mansfield Intensives
- Rutgers Summer Conservatory
- Southeastern Summer Theater Institute (SSTI)
- Stagedoor Manor
- Stella Adler Teen Summer Conservatory
- Syracuse University, Summer College
- Texas State University, NEXUS Musical Theatre Pre-College Intensive
- UCLA, Acting and Performance Summer Institute
- University of Cincinnati, College Conservatory of Music
- University of Michigan, MPulse Summer Performing Arts Institutes
- University of North Carolina School of the Arts
- University of Southern California High School Summer Conservatory
- Walnut Hill School for the Arts

FESTIVAL JOBS AND INTERNSHIPS

ALABAMA

Alabama Shakespeare Festival
Location: Montgomery, AL
Career Opportunities: Positions open as available across the spectrum of theatre positions.[2]

CALIFORNIA

Marin Shakespeare Festival
Location: San Rafael, CA (Dominican University)
Paid Positions:[3] Stage Manager, Assistant Stage Manager, Carpenters, Costume Designers, Costume Assistants, House Manager/Assistant House Manager, Lighting Designer, Master Carpenter, Master Electrician, Prop Designer, Scenic Painters, Set Designer, and Wardrobe Supervisor
Volunteer Positions:[4] Carpenters / Scenic Painters, Costume Helpers, Dressers,

---

2   Alabama Shakespeare Festival, "Career Opportunities," *Alabama Shakespeare Festival*, n.d., https://asf.net/careers/

3   Marin Shakespeare Company, "Job Openings," *Marin Shakespeare Company*, n.d., https://www.marinshakespeare.org/jobs/

4   Idaho Shakespeare Festival, "Volunteer," *Idaho Shakespeare Festival*, n.d., https://idahoshakespeare.org/volunteer/

Technicians, Sound and Light Operators, and Ushers

Shakespeare Santa Cruz
Location: Santa Cruz, CA (University of California, Santa Cruz)
Internships: The summer season opens for intern applications in late fall and closes in February. Applications will be reviewed in February.[5] For more information, contact intern@santacruzshakespeare.org

Will Geer Theatricum Botanicum
Location: Topanga, CA
Internships:[6] Acting, administration, technical design, education and production – we have an internship for every aspect of Theatricum's operation.

COLORADO

Colorado Shakespeare Festival
Location: Boulder, CO (University of Colorado, Boulder)
Positions/Internships: For positions as they open, see https://cupresents.org/about-cu-presents/job-opportunities/

Creede Repertory Theatre
Location: Creede, CO
Professional Positions:[7] Numerous positions are open for each summer form May – July, including stage management, technical, carpentry, costume, first hand, sound, lighting, electrician, artisan, paint, props, and stitcher.

CONNECTICUT

Goodspeed Musicals
Location: East Haddam, CT
Paid Production Apprenticeships: Positions are available in Stage Carpentry, Technical/Construction, Prop Run Crew, Costume Shop, Stitchers, Wardrobe, and Electrics. Most 2022 apprenticeship positions are paid minimum wage. To apply, submit cover letter, resume, availability and list of three references to jobs@goodspeed.org.[8]

---

5   Santa Cruz Shakespeare, "Internship," *Santa Cruz Shakespeare*, n.d., https://santacruzshakespeare.org/internship/

6   Will Geer's Theatricum Botanicum, "Internships," *Will Geer's Theatricum Botanicum*, n.d., https://theatricum.com/internships/

7   Creede Repertory Theatre, "Work With Us," *Creede Repetory Theatre*, n.d., https://creederep.org/work-with-us/

8   Goodspeed Musicals, "Job Opportunities," *Goodspeed Musicals,* n.d., https://www.goodspeed.org/about/career-opportunities

IDAHO

Idaho Shakespeare Festival
Location: Boise, ID
Volunteer/Paid/Apprenticeship Positions: Production & Technical Positions, Volunteers, Apprenticeship Program, Workshops, Residences, Casting, Directors & Designers, and Acting Company.

ILLINOIS

Illinois Shakespeare Festival
Location: Bloomington, IL (Illinois State University)
Internships: Acting, Company Management, Lighting/Electrics, Prop Shop, Scenic Artist/Paint Shop, Scene Shop/Carpentry, Sound Shop, and Stage Management. "Interns will participate in an internship class once a week for professional development and education. Interns will be registered for THE 398 - Professional Practice in Theatre at Illinois State University…The Illinois Shakespeare Festival will pay for the tuition and fees for up to six credit hours of THE 398 and assist students in transferring this credit to their home academic institution.

"Our summer 2022 course will be facilitated by Dr. Ann Haugo and Dr. Derek R. Munson. Interns will meet with their mentor and the production manager every three weeks. Mentorship meeting goals are to provide structured feedback for each individual, discuss any programmatic challenges they are having, and to set goals for the internship experience.

"Current enrollment in a college program with an anticipated graduation date of August 2022 or later. Ability to commit to the full summer season. All internships are full-time commitments."[9]

MAINE

Theater at Monmouth
Location: Monmouth, ME
Internships: "Each year, early career theatre artists, technicians, and administrators start their professional journey at Theater at Monmouth. Members of the intern and apprentice company work alongside artists and professionals to produce the summer season at one of the nation's only classical repertory theatre."[10]

---

9   Illinois Shakespeare Festival, "Internship Program," *Illinois Shakespeare Festival*, n.d., https://illinoisshakes. com/employment/internships/

10   Theater at Monmouth, "Work With Us," *Theater at Monmouth*, n.d., http://theateratmonmouth.org/about-us/ work-with-us/

28

MASSACHUSETTS

Barrington Stage Company
Location: Pittsfield, MA
Internships/Jobs:[11] The listing in early 2022 included these positions: Lighting and Sound Technician, Scene Shop Operations Manager, Scenic Carpenter/Welder, Scenic Carpenter, Charge Scenic Artist, Scenic Artist, Stitcher, Associate Wardrobe Supervisor, Wardrobe Technician, Light Board Operator, Electrician, Audio Supervisor, Sound Board Operator (A1), Sound Technician (A2), Properties Supervisor, Assistant Properties Supervisor, Properties Artisan, Stage Crew Chief, Stage Crew.

Berkshire Theater Festival
Location: Pittsfield/Stockbridge, MA
Internships and Jobs: https://www.berkshiretheatregroup.org/Join%20Our%20Team/#Year-Round_Job_Opps

Shakespeare & Company
Location: Lenox, MA
Internships: In addition to exclusive lectures, career guidance, and the possibility of a capstone project, "Interns receive one-on-one mentoring from within their department and experience with professional artists and staff…Internships are available year-round, typically 15- or 16-week duration, but if one of the tracks below is not perfect for an applicant, programs of custom duration or areas of interest can be developed as well."[12]

Williamstown Theatre Festival
Location: Williamstown, MA (Williams College)
Internships: "Tony Award-winning Williamstown Theatre Festival's summer season offers a variety of career opportunities for theatre professionals at all levels of experience…. In the summer of 2021, salaried positions will be compensated at a range of $684 to $750 per week. Hourly positions will be compensated at a rate of $13.50 to $15.00 per hour."[13]

NEW YORK

Adirondack Theatre Festival
Location: Glen Falls, NY
Internships: "ATF's professional internship program offers rigorous, hands-on educational opportunities for current students and early career professionals seeking an introduction to careers in the professional theatre. Our goal is to

---

11   Barrington Stage Company, "Job Opportunities," *Barrington Stage Company,* n.d., https://barringtonstageco.org/about-the-company/jobs/

12   Shakespeare & Company, "Jobs and Volunteering," *Shakespeare & Company,* n.d., https://www.shakespeare.org/jobs-and-volunteering/interns

13   Williamstown Theatre Festival, "Work & Learn," *Williamstown Theatre Festival,* n.d., https://wtfestival.org/work-learn/

provide interns with practical experience in the shop, rehearsal room, backstage and in the front office as well as valuable networking opportunities with working theatre professionals."[14] Internships available in administration, artistic, production, carpentry, electrics, sound, props, paint, and wardrobe.

Apply by February 1st. Chorus roles are possible for interns as well. "While interns are assigned specific departments and mentors, they are also expected to learn and work outside their chosen area of expertise. We hope to provide the intern with a well-rounded experience designed to inform them of all the various jobs required to mount a professional production." Interns may receive either course credit or a weekly stipend.

Hudson Valley Shakespeare Festival
Location: Garrison, NY
Internships/Training: "While most theater training programs are unpaid (or charge tuition), we're proud to pay educational stipends to participants and, in most cases, offer local housing, reducing barriers to employment in the arts. Our Conservatory Company training program, Production and Administrative Internships and Directing Fellowships offer exceptional practical experience through collaboration, hands-on learning, and mentorship."[15]

Powerhouse Theater
Location: Poughkeepsie, NY (Vassar College)
Training Program: The summer 2022 training program is five weeks encompassing the theatre process while observing and participating in shows.[16]

Shakespeare in the Park
Location: New York, NY
Freelance Positions: Stitchers/Costume Department – stitching and finishes to costumes - $25/hour
Scenery Department – Hard-working carpenters, scenic artists, and props run crew. Construction/painting experience required - $25-$27/hour.[17]

OREGON

Oregon Shakespeare Festival
Location: Ashland, OR
Internships: "Internships are designed to provide participants with a learning

---

14 Adirondack Theatre Festival, "Professional Theatre Internships at Adirondack Theatre Festival," *Adirondack Theatre Festival*, 2021, https://www.atfestival.org/opportunities/internships/

15 Hudson Valley Shakespeare Festival, "Professional Training," *Hudson Valley Shakespeare Festival*, n.d., https://hvshakespeare.org/education/training/

16 Vassar College, "Powerhouse Theater Training Program," *Vassar College*, n.d., https://www.vassar.edu/powerhouse/apprentices/

17 The Public, "Employment & Internships," *The Public*, n.d., https://publictheater.org/footer/employment--internships/

opportunity within our artistic, production, and administration areas...Prior theatre experience is not required. This is a 2- to 4–month experience that is designed to provide a professional development opportunity for emerging artists and aspiring arts administrators. Recipients are paired with an OSF company member and receive mentorship in their respective discipline.

"Internships are unpaid learning opportunities. Housing and travel are not provided for Internships...Candidates for Internships must be a high school graduate or have at least one year of work experience. Applicants interested in an Internship in Stage Management and any of the production areas must have at least one year of experience in their specific area of interest, a year of experience in an academic environment will be considered."[18]

PENNSYLVANIA

Pennsylvania Shakespeare Festival
Location: Center Valley, PA
The 2022 Season includes productions of A Chorus Line, Fences, Little Red, Every Brilliant Thing, The River Bride (reading) and Much Ado About Nothing.
Internships: There are numerous Stage Management (SM) tracks. Interns work alongside Equity SMs. Responsibilities include prop tracking, feeding lines, backstage deck, run crew, lifting, props, repairing, construction, carpentry, and foreman shadowing. Specialty skills will be learned on the job. SM and Carp intern positions must go-getters in a fast-paced environment. Salary $300/week.
Costume Design – First Hand Assistant to the Cutter/Draper – Experienced in pattern layout/cutting/sewing. Salary $475/week. **Costume Shop Craftsperson** – assists with crafts, including millinery, footwear, jewelry, masks – must be self-motivated, manage multiple simultaneous projects. and able to read/interpret sketches. Salary $425/week. **Stitcher** – Intermediate/Advanced sewing by hand/maching, including alterations, construction, and finishing. Salary $340/week. **Costume Shop Intern** and **Costume Shop Management Intern** – Assists the costumer design staff while working following instructions and working independently. Salary $300/week. **Wardrobe Crafts** and **Wardrobe Stitcher**– Salary $340/week. **Wardrobe Intern** and **Wig and Makeup Dresser** – Salary $300/week

TEXAS

Texas Shakespeare Festival
Location: Kilgore, TX (Kilgore College)
Internships:[19]
Costume Intern / Wardrobe: May 20 - August 3   Salary: $1,500 / double occupancy dorm housing / 14 meals a week. Minimum Requirements: undergraduate costume

18   Oregon Shakespeare Festival, "Internships," *Oregon Shakespeare Festival*, n.d., https://www.osfashland.org/en/work-with-us/FAIR/Internships.aspx

19   Texas Shakespeare Festival, "Costume Department," *Texas Shakespeare Festival*, n.d., https://www.texasshakespeare.com/costumes

technology training required and/or one year of professional experience. **Costume and Wig Stylist Intern:** May 20 - August 3 Salary: $1,500 / double occupancy dormitory housing / 14 meals a week. Minimum Requirements: undergraduate training in wigs and hairstyling preferred and/or one year of professional experience working on wigs and hairstyling. **Properties Intern:** May 20 - August 3 Salary: $1,500 stipend / double occupancy dorm housing / 14 meals a week Note: Properties Interns are assigned primarily to the properties department, but may also be reassigned, as needed, to other technical areas. **Scenic Carpenters:** May 16 - August 3 Salary: $4,400 stipend / up to $300 / double occupancy dorm housing / 14 meals a week Minimum Requirements: Experience with various scenic construction techniques and materials; strong woodworking skills. **Scene Painting Intern:** May 20 - August 3 Salary: $1,500 stipend / double occupancy dorm housing / 14 meals a week. Minimum Requirements: Fundamental experience in scenic treatments including, but not limited to, faux finish, carving, texturing, aging, and distressing. The candidate should also be comfortable working at heights above 16'. **Lighting Intern:** May 20 - August 3   Salary: $1,500 stipend / double occupancy dorm housing / 14 meals a week. Minimum Requirements: Assist with the hang, focus, and strike of electrics and special effects for all productions; program and run the lighting console for shows as assigned; assist with the maintenance and upkeep for all lighting inventory and systems. **Stage Management Intern**: May 20 - August 3 Salary: $1,500 stipend / double occupancy dorm housing / 14 meals a week. Minimum requirement: one year undergraduate stage management training. **Stage Management Intern:** May 20 - August 3 Salary: $1,500 stipend / double occupancy dorm housing / 14 meals a week. Minimum Requirement: minimum one year undergraduate stage management training.

UTAH

Utah Shakespearean Festival
Location: Cedar City, UT
Inernships: May/June – July/September Draper:[20] May – July - Oversees all construction of costumes for assigned show. Works in direct relationship with costume designer. **First Hand:** Works with the draper to construct and supervise construction of costumes. Supervises costume technicians. **Technician:** Constructs all costume pieces assigned by first hand. Contracts are May 2–July 2 or June 1–July 13. **Wardrobe:** Works on the run of assigned productions assisting in preparation and maintenance (laundry and repair) of costumes. **Assistant Costume Crafts Supervisor:** Assists with the operation of costume crafts including scheduling of fittings and attending fittings; helps interpret costume designer's sketches and ideas and assists with problem-solving and engineering of costume crafts items. **Crafts Technician:** Assists senior crafts technician in the construction of all accessories or special costume projects. **Junior Artisan/Stage Crew:** Responsible for the building and fabrication of stage and rehearsal properties for assigned productions. Works with the prop team to complete shop improvement

---

20   Utah Shakespeare Festival, "Employment," *Utah Shakespeare Festival*, n.d., https://www.bard.org/employment

and organizational projects as assigned. **Scenic Carpenter**: Constructs and loads in all scenic set elements for assigned productions. Completes shop improvement and organization projects as assigned. **Junior Carpenter/Stage Crew:** Constructs and loads-in all scenic set elements for assigned productions. Responsible for running, storage, and maintenance of scenery for assigned productions. **Scenic Artist:** Responsible for painting and finishing of all scenic elements for assigned productions. **Junior Painter/Stage Crew:** Responsible for painting and finishing of all scenic elements for assigned productions. Responsible for running, storage, and maintenance of paints for assigned productions. **Deck Carpenter:** Responsible for load in, running, organization of storage, and maintenance of scenery and props for a theatre (Engelstad, Randall, or Anes). Works with scenery director on stage crew schedule and necessary adjustments. **Junior Carpenters/Painters/Prop Interns:** Responsible for load in, running, storage, changeovers, and maintenance of scenery and props for assigned productions. **Stage Crew:** Responsible for load in, running, storage, and changeovers of scenery and props for assigned productions.

VIRGINIA

American Shakespeare Center
Location: Staunton, VA
Drama Club: "With Shakespeare's text as our touchstone and his technology as our laboratory, the Drama Club meets once a week in 12-week terms to explore Shakespeare's wordcraft and stagecraft through play, building confidence and expanding creativity by working together to craft and rehearse a final performance of Shakespearean scenes at the Blackfriars Playhouse."[21]

Appalachian Festival of Plays and Playwrights
Location: Abingdon, VA (Emory & Henry College -10 min away)
Internships: The Association of the Barter Theatre with Emory & Henry College "offers theatre majors opportunities for professional internships, mentoring, workshops, and master classes throughout their college career. Barter staff members and artists often serve as adjunct faculty and guest artists in the Theatre Department. In addition, E&H theatre majors have the opportunity to attend professional rehearsals, participate in "talk backs" with the actors and crew after Barter performances, and serve as understudies in Barter Theatre productions. With this partnership, Emory & Henry Theatre Department offers students the combined strengths of a small liberal arts college and the type of pre-professional experiences often found only in large conservatories."[22]

WEST VIRGINIA

Contemporary American Theater Festival
Location: Shepherdstown, WV (Shepherd University)

21 American Shakespeare Center, "Drama Club," *American Shakespeare Center,* n.d., https://americanshakespearecenter.com/education/drama-club/

22 Barter Theatre, "Emory & Henry College," *Barter Theatre,* n.d., https://bartertheatre.com/emory-henry/

Internships: "Apply for a specific department based on your strengths and passions as a theater artist. You may apply for no more than two departments [carpentry, costumes, electrics, props, scenic arts, sound] but if hired, you will only be assigned to one. Internships usually begin in late May and end in early August, running 8-10 weeks."[23]

WISCONSIN

American Players Theatre
Location: Spring Green, WI
Positions: Stitchers, Wigs, Stage Management, Carpentry, First Hand, Lighting, Production[24]

INTERNATIONAL

ONTARIO, CANADA

Shaw Festival
Location: Niagara-On-The-Lake, Ontario, Canada
Camps and Training Programs: While there are no internships, per se, there is training, including a summer stage combat class.

Stratford Shakespeare Festival
Location: Stratford, Ontario, Canada
Camps and Training Programs: While there are no internships, per se, there are summer camps and training programs for students of all ages.

---

23 Contemporary American Theater Festival, "Internships," *Contemporary American Theater Festival*, n.d., https://catf.org/internships/

24 American Players Theatre, "Employment," *American Players Theatre*, n.d., https://americanplayers.org/about/employment

CHAPTER 6

WHAT IS THE DIFFERENCE BETWEEN AA, AS, BA, BS, BFA, MFA?

"Wisdom is not a product of schooling but of the lifelong attempt to acquire it."

– Albert Einstein

UNDERGRADUATE AND GRADUATE DEGREES

AA – Associate of Arts – 2-year degree

AS – Associate of Science – 2-year degree

BA – Bachelor of Arts – 4-year degree

BS – Bachelor of Science – 4-year degree

BFA – Bachelor of Fine Arts – 4-year degree with most classes focused on art

MFA – Master of Fine Arts – 1-2-year degree earned after the BA, BS, or BFA

Basically, the BA and BS are degrees that typically offer a liberal arts foundation along with a major or concentration in a specific subject. Meanwhile, a BFA is considered a professional arts-focused degree with fewer courses in English, science, math, social science, and the humanities. Thus, the BFA is a specialist qualification in the arts. BA or BS degrees in fine arts, costume design, technical theatre, or drama degree are also valuable. The BFA focuses on the specific area of art you decide to choose.

The BA and BS degrees include significantly more liberal arts classes and thus are more general degrees. However, the intention of the BFA degree is for students to pursue an arts-focused curriculum and thus there are fewer general subject courses.

Finally, while many AA or AS degrees for costume design and technical theatre are focused on providing technical or professional skills, an AA or AS in these areas are often interchangeable. Similarly, a BA or BS in costume design or technical theatre are also relatively interchangeable. However, a BFA may be seen as being different than a BA or BS since there is typically more coursework focused on your specific pursuit. Thus, you may have more technical experiences and knowledge than someone who has a BA or BS.

AA – ASSOCIATE OF ARTS

The Associate of Arts degree is typically a 2-year general studies degree offered online or in-person by a community college. However, some universities offer AA degrees as well. The Associate of Arts degree focuses on liberal arts courses and often has no barrier to entry, meaning that students can enter most AA programs with a high school diploma or the equivalent. Some students take a longer or shorter time to complete the AA based upon their skills upon entering the program, certainty about the direction they are heading, and the transfer requirements for the program they desire. For example, students majoring in business may have additional business, communication, accounting, and economics requirements and need to create an academic plan early in their program to finish in two years.

AS – ASSOCIATE OF SCIENCE

The Associate of Science degree is very similar to the AA. However, the AS degree frequently emphasizes science and math and often has additional requirements.

BA – BACHELOR OF ARTS

The Bachelor of Arts degree is typically a 4-year degree offered online or in-person by a college or university. However, a few community colleges offer BA degrees as well. Some students complete their BA in fewer years depending upon AP/IB credit, dual enrollment in high school, and summer/intersession classes. Students apply to a college or university with stricter or less stringent requirements depending upon the school. The Bachelor of Arts degree frequently requires students to take lower-division (first and second year) liberal arts courses before taking specialized courses focused around a major or concentration in their third and fourth years. Some students take a longer or shorter time to complete their BA based upon their skills upon entering the program, certainty about the direction they are heading, and the chosen major. College advisors aid students in finishing "on time" though less than half of all students in the United States who start a BA program do not finish their degree in four years according to the National Center for Educational Statistics.[1]

BS – BACHELOR OF SCIENCE

The Bachelor of Science degree is very similar to the BA. However, the BS degree frequently emphasizes science and math and often has additional requirements.[2]

BFA – BACHELOR OF FINE ARTS

The Bachelor of Fine Arts is a 4-year college degree focusing on the arts. BFA students are often not required to take as many English, science, math, social

---

1   IEC NCES, "Digest of Education Statistics, Table 326.10," *IES NCES*, n.d., https://nces.ed.gov/programs/digest/d20/tables/dt20_326.10.asp?referer=raceindica.asp

2   IEC NCES, "Digest of Education Statistics, Table 326.10," *IES NCES*, n.d., https://nces.ed.gov/programs/digest/d20/tables/dt20_326.10.asp?referer=raceindica.asp

science, and humanities courses. Students must still complete roughly the same number of credits as a person who earns a BA or BS and the courses are not necessarily easier. BFA students frequently take general art requirements to lay a foundation in drawing, graphic design, and courses in their specialty area by completing their first two years along with basic writing and quantitative skill-building. BFA students are traditionally art-in-practice students who learn the technical craft of their art form while putting in enormous numbers of hours practicing their skill assignments and participating in internships and experiential learning. Students who know that they want a future in the arts often find this avenue perfectly tailored for their pursuits. However, students who change their minds and transfer to a university in another degree program may require an additional year to make up for coursework they have not completed.

MFA – MASTER OF FINE ARTS

The Master of Fine Arts is a graduate degree for students who have completed their BA, BS, or BFA. This degree takes one to two years depending upon the program, coursework, and experiential component, which may be a capstone, practicum, internship, or thesis. While there are also MA and MS degrees, many art students who continue on to earn their master's degree in the arts choose to focus on their field of interest. The MFA is an intensive immersion into a higher level of skill-building. However, students who graduate with an MFA have a broader range of talents and experiences than those who earn their bachelor's degrees. While admission into these programs is generally selective, with planning, preparation, and a good portfolio, there are many college options to pursue your interests.

THE SEVEN MAJOR DIFFERENCES BETWEEN THE ASSOCIATE, BACHELORS, AND MASTER'S DEGREES

1. Starting Point
2. Academic Discipline
3. Time to Completion
4. Location of the Education
5. Educational Costs
6. Earning Power
7. Professional Opportunities

STARTING POINT

Most students who begin with an Associate of Arts (AA) or Associate of Science (AS) have no college credits. Starting from scratch with their college education, they accumulate 60+ units at a community college starting point. Although students can transfer with less than 60 credits, an AA or AS degree requires 60 units. While most students earn AA or AS degrees at a community college, some earn this degree at a 4-year college or university.

The AA or AS is either a terminal degree, meaning that the student will not continue on with their bachelor's degree, or just a stepping stone to their BA, BS, or BFA. The difference between the associate's and bachelor's degrees is just the starting point.

The starting point for students who pursue a bachelor's degree may be farther along the traditional 4-year pathway. Meanwhile, the starting point for the master's degree (MA, MS, or MFA) begins after obtaining a bachelor's degree.

ACADEMIC DISCIPLINE

Every degree encompasses different requirements. Requirements for the AA are different than an AS. Similarly, the requirements for the BA, BS, and BFA also differ. With two additional years of coursework, the BA, BS, and BFA is more thorough. The MA, MS, and MFA build upon the bachelor's degree and even deeper. Costume design students will not take the same classes as students in technical theatre, though there may be a few that overlap. Though both are behind the scenes in theatre or film, the essential skills and course requirements for each career area are distinct.

Furthermore, with the myriad of combinations, it is rare that any two undergraduate students have the same exact classes in the same exact order. Just as the requirements for a chemistry degree are not the same as for a biology degree, a graphic design degree also differs greatly from a fashion design degree. Various degrees not only include a different number of credits but different types of classes and program specifications.

TIME TO COMPLETION

Associate of Arts (AA) and Associate of Science (AS) degrees typically take two years, while most BA, BS, and BFA degrees are 4-year programs, depending upon full-time or part-time status. Students who transfer in credits or earn credits otherwise can reduce their time to completion.

Some students may choose to extend their education in costume design or technical theatre by earning a second bachelor's degree in another field. By cross-training, students open more doors. For example, a degree in business at the bachelor's level or a Master's in Business Administration (MBA) may offer more options for future leadership positions.

Time in college can be reduced with credits earned in high school. Some students enter a BA, BS, or BFA program having already completed college credits because they were dual-enrolled or they took college classes directly through a college or university ahead of time. Some students have taken AP/IB tests from taking higher-level tests while in high school and earned qualifying scores to be granted credits by the college or university. Other ways students can enter at a different starting point are with credit-by-exam, CLEP tests, experiential credits, and those granted in the military.

Colleges and universities are keenly aware of the challenges students face today with work, illness, and family responsibilities. Thus, many schools of higher education offer flexible enrollment with opportunities for part-time, evening, weekend, and online classes.

LOCATION OF THE EDUCATION

The AA and AS are earned at colleges that grant 2-year degrees. The location may be at a local community college or a university. BA, BS, and BFA programs are offered at a 4-year college or university. However, with online classes, students have the flexibility to take classes from colleges farther away as well. Thus, the location in which a typical student studies is not as set as it once was.

Nevertheless, the production of dramas, musicals, and films are often in fixed locations. Since most of these require a physical location, during the pandemic, many film programs adjusted by having students create films at home and theatre students created monologues and virtual readings. Most colleges and universities from the 2-year degree to graduate school offer theatre of some sort and thus, those with skills in costume design and technical theatre are needed and the experience can add to a student's portfolio.

EDUCATIONAL COSTS

Since the AA or AS requires a shorter amount of time and is typically completed at a lower-cost community college, the cost for an associate's degree is typically less than a bachelor's degree. Master's degree programs often cost more per credit, but take less time than a bachelor's degree.

On the other hand, many students can obtain financial aid in the form of grants, loans, and both merit and need-based scholarships. This aid can go far in paying for school and reducing debt after college.

EARNING POWER

Students with more education can earn more. According to the 2019 National Center for Educational Statistics (NCES) data for median salaries,[3]

Master's Degree or Higher - $70,000
Bachelor's Degree - $55,700
Associate's Degree - $43,300
High School - $35,000

PROFESSIONAL OPPORTUNITIES

Earning a BA, BS, or BFA opens more doors than an AA or AS. Similarly, an MA, MS, or MFA opens more doors than a BA, BS, or BFA. Companies typically seek employees with greater knowledge and professional experience. However, the caveat to this is that some companies do not want to pay more for those with more education but less experience. Training takes up much of a company's budget. When entering professional theatre, there are numerous technical, software, and communication skills required. A nimble technician or costume designer contributes most when they have soft skills, like creativity, collaboration, and self-motivation.

---

3   IES NCES, "Annual Earnings by Educational Attainment," *IEC NCES,* May 2021, https://nces.ed.gov/programs/coe/indicator/cba

Nevertheless, theatres have the dual challenge to have the manpower to put on a great show while also keeping the budget down so that they can afford to continue producing shows. While colleges promote and develop skills and competencies, theatres need to cut down the learning curve when entering a position. This is best done by bringing in experienced talent. Thus, a student with a BFA sometimes has more experience than one with a BA or BS, though there are plenty of students with BA and BS degrees who built a portfolio of knowledge by starting early. Also, they may have a broader liberal arts sense to interpret plays, musicals, and films.

CHAPTER 7

COSTUME DESIGN: DEGREES AND REQUIREMENTS

"The only way to do our best work right now, is to work well together."

– Tim Carl

Costume design requires more than envisioning and drawing a costume. Costume designers must be skilled seamstresses and stitchers. Becoming an expert in sewing is a must. Most costume design programs are rigorous. Furthermore, pattern making requires mathematical skills as well as graphic design to lay out and replicate patterns for various sizes. Costume design school will teach the workflow, production patterns, construction techniques, and finishing methodologies used in the industry.

Thus, the first three necessary skills are centered around creativity, drawing, and sewing. However, college degrees in costume design teach much more. Some of those skills include manually working with a live fit model, specialized cutting techniques with different kinds of scissors and hand stitching types for seams, hems, and crafting.

Costume design school will teach you skills for stage and film, such as breaking down characters from a script and conceptualizing their identities by developing a look book using mood boards, color stories, and illustrations. Creativity and ingenuity provide the fit within the historical period, theme, and emotional context. This exploration and idea generation entails stretching your mind by watching shows of all types and imagining what you would do to enhance the audience's emotions by using costuming to understand the character's experience.

Keep a small notebook with you to jot down inspiration as you witness ups and downs throughout your life's experiences.

At the beginning of the inspiration for this book, the plan was to only include profiles of the top twenty schools for costume design. However, every list seemed different, and everyone interviewed had a new college to add or a good reason why a school should be included. Thus, the profile section has approximately fifty schools. Nevertheless, there are some schools that traditionally rank in the top lists. Here is one of those lists.

According to the *Hollywood Reporter*, the top ten schools for Costume Design are:

1. California Institute of the Arts (CalArts)
2. Carnegie Mellon School of Drama
3. NYU Tisch School of the Arts
4. Savannah College of Art and Design (SCAD)
5. UCLA School of Theater, Film, and Television
6. The University of Missouri – Kansas City (UMKC)

7. Wimbledon College of Arts, University of the Arts London (UAL)
8. University of North Carolina School of the Arts (UNSCA)
9. USC School of Dramatic Arts
10. Yale School of Drama

FAMOUS COSTUME DESIGNERS

Edith Head: won 8 Academy Awards; 35 nominations
College: BA University of California, Berkeley in French;
MA Stanford University in Roman Languages

Milena Canonero: won 4 Academy Awards; 9 nominations
Studied art, design history, and costume design in Genoa

Colleen Atwood: won 4 Academy Awards; 12 nominations
College: Cornish College of the Arts in Painting

Irene Sharaff: won 5 Academy Awards; 15 nominations
College: Parsons School of Design
Art Students League of New York
Académie de la Grande Chaumière in Paris

Charles Le Maire: won 3 Academy Awards; 13 nominations

Sandy Powell: won 3 Academy Awards; 15 nominations
College: Central School of Art and Design in Theatre Design

Dorothy Jeakins: won 3 Academy Awards; 12 nominations

College: Otis College of Art and Design

Anthony Powell: won 3 Academy Awards; 6 nominations

College: Central School of Art and Design

TONY AWARD NOMINATED COSTUME DESIGNERS FOR A MUSICAL (2010 – 2020)

Greg Barnes for *Follies* (2012), *Kinky Boots* (2013), *Something Rotten!* (2015), *Tuck Everlasting* (2016), *Mean Girls* (2018)

Tim Chappel for *Priscilla, Queen of the Desert* (2011)

Linda Cho for *A Gentleman's Guide to Love and Murder* (2014), *Anastasia* (2017)

Bob Crowley for *An American in Paris* (2015)

Marina Draghici for *Fela!* (2010)

Lizzy Gardiner for *Priscilla, Queen of the Desert* (2011)

Rob Howell for *Matilda the Musical* (2013)

Eiko Ishioka for *Spider-Man: Turn Off the Dark* (2012)

Michael Krass for *Hadestown* (2019)

Dominique Lemieux *for Pippin* (2013)

William Ivey Long for *Rogers and Hammerstein's Cinderella* (2013), *Bullets Over Broadway* (2014), *On the Twentieth Century* (2015), *Beetlejuice* (2019), *Tootsie* (2019)

Santo Loquasto for *Hello Dolly!* (2017)

Bob Mackie for *The Cher Show* (2019)

Jeff Mahshie for *She Loves Me* (2016)

Martin Pakledinaz for *Anything Goes* (2011), *Nice Work If You Can Get It* (2012)

Arianne Phillips for *Hedwig and the Angry Inch* (2014)

Clint Ramos for *Once on This Island* (2018)

Emily Rebholz for *Jagged Little Pill* (2020)

Ann Roth for *The Book of Mormon* (2011), *Shuffle Along* (2016), *Carousel* (2018)

Emilio Sosa for *Porgy and Bess* (2012)

Paul Tazewell for *Memphis* (2010), *Hamilton* (2016), *Ain't Too Proud* (2019)

Mark Thompson for *Tina* (2020)

Isabel Toledo for *After Midnight* (2014)

Matthew Wright for *La Cage aux Folles* (2010)

Paloma Young for *Natasha, Pierre & The Great Comet of 1812* (2017)

David Zinn for *SpongeBob SquarePants* (2018)

Catherine Zuber for *How to Succeed in Business Without Really Trying* (2011), *The King and I* (2015), *War Paint* (2017), *My Fair Lady (2018)*, *Moulin Rouge!* (2020)

TONY AWARD NOMINATED COSTUME DESIGNERS FOR A PLAY
(2010 – 2020)

Dede Ayite for *Slave Play* (2020), *A Soldier's Play* (2020)

Bob Crowley for *The Audience* (2015), *The Inheritance* (2020)

Johnson Fensom for *Farinelli and the King* (2018)

Nicky Gillibrand for *Angels in America* (2018)

Soutra Gilmour for *Cyrano de Bergerac* (2013)

Jess Goldstein for *The Merchant of Venice* (2011)

Jane Greenwood for *Act One* (2014), *You Can't Take It with You* (2015), *Long Day's Journey into Night* (2016), *Little Foxes* (2017)

Desmond Heeley for *The Importance of Being Earnest* (2011)

Susan Hilferty for *Present Laughter* (2017)

Rob Howell for *The Ferryman* (2019)

Toni-Leslie James for *Jitney* (2017), *Bernhardt/Hamlet* (2019)

Michael Krass for *Machinal* (2014), *Noises Off* (2016)

Katrina Lindsay for *Harry Potter and the Cursed Child* (2018)

William Ivey Long for *Don't Dress for Dinner* (2012)

Christopher Oram for *Wolf Hall Parts One & Two* (2015)

Martin Pakledinaz for *Lend Me a Tenor* (2010)

Clint Ramos for *Eclipsed* (2016), *Torch Song* (2019), *The Rose Tattoo* (2020)

Constanza Romero for *Fences* (2010)

Ann Roth for *The Nance* (2013), *Three Tall Women* (2018), *The Iceman Cometh* (2018), *To Kill a Mockingbird* (2019), *Gary: A Sequel to Titus Andronicus* (2019)

Rita Ryack for *Casa Valentina* (2014)

Tom Scutt for *King Charles III* (2016)

Paul Tazewell for *A Streetcar Named Desire* (2012), *Hamilton* (2016), *Ain't Too Proud* (2019)

Mark Thompson for *La Bete* (2011), *One Man, Two Guvnors* (2012)

Jenny Tiramani for *Twelfth Night* (2014)

Albert Wolsky for *The Heiress* (2013)

Paloma Young for *Peter and the Starcatcher* (2012)

David Zinn for *In the Next Room (or The Vibrator Play)* (2010), *Airline Highway* (2015), *A Doll's House, Part 2* (2017)

Catherine Zuber for *The Royal Family* (2010), *Born Yesterday* (2011), *Golden Boy* (2013)

CHAPTER 8

TECHNICAL THEATRE: DEGREES AND REQUIREMENTS

"We work hard. We laugh. We cry. We rush around. We work late nights. We network with many people. We try our best to please everyone. We own at least 2 billion cables. We love what we do. We never give up. We are dedicated. We are technicians."

– Anonymous

G reat singers hypnotize. Talented dancers dazzle. Captivating actors mesmerize. Performers come to life in an impressive backdrop as singers, dancers, and actors enthrall audiences. With the stage set, actors appear, adorned in detailed costume designs. The visual spectacle appears centerstage with simple sets like "Music and the Mirror" in *A Chorus Line* or more complex designs like the barricade of chairs, tables, and boxes in *Les Misérables*.

Yet, the designs are just part of the work of technical theatre, which most people involved call a grueling and exhausting job. Celebrating afterward behind the curtains, the crew, wiped out, cheer for a job well down, while the singers, dancers, and actors take their bows to the audience. What draws students to technical theatre is the overwhelming sense of accomplishment the stage crew feels when the show is over and they hear the resounding reverberation of clapping and cheering from the crowd. Most say that nothing is more rewarding.

Nevertheless, mishaps occasionaly occur, like missing a stair and grabbing a ladder for mercy, hammering a nail partway into a finger, or barely getting a set out of the way before the curtains go up. Outside of the minor challenges and drops of spilled blood, most crew members keep going. First aid knowledge is a must. Keep soap, warm water, alcohol wipe, cotton ball, and sterilized tweezers or a needle handy to remove the occasional splinter. Fortunately, accidents are not common – it's all in a day's work.

Digital skills are enhanced and developed in a technical theatre program. Graphic design using Adobe Creative Cloud (Photoshop, Illustrator, InDesign, Premiere Pro, Acrobat, etc.) is one area of study. However, additional skills are required in order to create scale models, renderings, scale construction drawings, and the like. It could also include AutoCAD, 3DS Max, Revit, or Sketchup.

According to *College Raptor*, in 2022 the top ten technical theatre programs are:

1. University of North Carolina School of the Arts (UNSCA)
2. California Institute of the Arts (CalArts)
3. SUNY Purchase College
4. Savannah College of Art and Design (SCAD)
5. University of Cincinnati
6. University of Arizona
7. Boston University
8. Cornish College of the Arts
9. DePaul University
10. Emerson College

While this list may have one school higher or lower each year, this list is a good start and there a few dozen more that I have profiled in the back of this book.

TONY AWARD WINNERS FOR BEST SCENIC DESIGN IN A MUSICAL (2010-2020)

Christine Jones for *American Idiot* (2010)

Scott Pask for *The Book of Mormon* (2011)

Bob Crowley for *Once* (2012)

Rob Howell for *Matilda the Musical* (2013)

Christopher Barreca for *Rocky the Musical* (2014)

Bob Crowley & 59 Productions for *An American in Paris* (2015)

David Rockwell for *She Loves Me* (2016)

Mimi Lien for *Natasha, Pierre & The Great Comet of 1812* (2017)

David Zinn for *SpongeBob Square Pants* (2018)

Rachel Hauck for *Hadestown* (2019)

Derek McLane for *Moulin Rouge!* (2020)

TONY AWARD WINNERS FOR BEST SCENIC DESIGN IN A PLAY (2010-2020)

Christopher Oram for *Red* (2010)

Rae Smith for *War Horse* (2011)

Donyale Werle for *Peter and the Starcatcher* (2012)

John Lee Beatty for *The Nance* (2013)

Beowulf Boritt for *Act One* (2014)

Bunny Christie and Finn Ross for T*he Curious Incident of the Dog in the Night-Time* (2015)

David Zinn for *The Humans* (2016)

Nigel Hook for *The Play That Goes Wrong* (2017)

Christine Jones for *Harry Potter and the Cursed Child* (2018)

Rob Howell for *The Ferryman* (2019), *A Christmas Carol* (2020)

CHAPTER 9

COLLEGE ADMISSIONS: COURSEWORK REQUIREMENTS, SKILLS, AND SCHOLARSHIPS

"Theatre is a form of knowledge; it should and can also be a means of transforming society. Theatre can help us build our future, rather than just waiting for it."

– Augusto Boal

College admissions is a huge topic, and no treatment here will suffice to provide all of the nuances of the process. Students must apply by submitting the Common Application, Coalition Application, or specialized application for individual schools. Many schools of art, theatre, fashion, dance, voice, film, architecture, etc. require a portfolio. This is not true across the board and even within a discipline like theatre, some majors may require a portfolio while others do not.

Colleges want to get to know you. They can contact you with your name, address, phone number, e-mail address, and family information. They can learn a bit more with your school, grades, and test scores if required. They can interpret your interests through your activities, honors and awards, and a resume. They can take a better look at how you write, what you think, and what you determine is important to tell them through your essays. Finally, they can get an idea of what other people think about you, though you self-select those who you think will write the best testimonials of your attitude, talent, performance, leadership, communication, collaboration, motivation, discipline, and interests. However, no matter how much information you provide, a college application is rather static.

Dynamism is brought out through videos, skill areas, interviews, and auditions. Portfolios can be extremely valuable to a school. Preparation is necessary, albeit time-consuming. I find that some of the most talented people I have worked with put less time into the portfolio because they are so busy being great at everything they do. Thus, some of the best candidates wait until the last minute to work on their applications, essays, resumes, and portfolio materials. However, college admissions officers seek the best talent from what they know and what you send. Your presentation makes a significant difference. They can often see around the corners to find greatness, but it is best if you put the time into putting your best foot forward.

Admissions dates vary. Furthermore, due to the time it takes to evaluate an applicant, due dates for artistic candidates are often sooner than you expect and before other admissions applications. Thus, not only are there extra requirements, the dates are earlier. Scholarship due dates are early too. While you can apply for financial aid using the Free Application for Federal Student Aid (FAFSA) and College Scholarship Service (CSS Profile), scholarships are offered by individual institutions. These scholarships are often worth $100,000 or more over the course of four years. The money they offer can make your entire college experience easier to manage.

The pandemic threw a wrench into the flywheel of admissions. Many changes were made on the inside of the college's decision-making process, though some were also made on the student-facing side. The uncertainty about who would come, whether they would defer, and what kind of education would be delivered required deferrals, waitlists, and questions about programs. More students applied to the top schools, though some schools witnessed a decrease in applications. Many students chose to apply Early Decision, Early Action, and Restricted Early Action to top schools.

COLLEGE ADMISSIONS:

Success in the Face of Uncertainty

There are no guarantees in college admissions. However, planning is essential for success. The most beneficial advice is to pursue your passions with gusto, train to be the best you can be, take advantage of internships and experiences, and meet lots of people along the way. Remember, "life is a journey, not a destination." Often the journey is more exciting, leading to lessons, friendships, and indelible moments. However, the fact is…in the end, if college is your goal, there are a few action items you need to remember to be successful in the admissions process.

Should you worry about grades? Of course. You should also take classes that will challenge you. Colleges pick the best candidates from those who apply. Students must be academically prepared, socially conscious, and especially talented in a few different areas in which they are passionate (conceptual design, graphic arts, costumes, theater, acting, singing, dance, musical instruments, debate, public speaking, leadership, athletics, community service, computer coding, robotics, construction, etc.).

This selection process is no different than companies picking from the best team members in a company to create a successful employee dynamic. While colleges are more or less competitive, companies may have only one job and fifty resumes. Discover the unique drive and internal motivations within you that make you the very best you can be. Be exceptional at what you choose to do academically, personally, and professionally.

Most of all,

You Do You!

TALENT FOCUSED

Not all schools require high grades and test scores. Many are simply interested in selecting students who are the most talented, most driven, and the most willing to be team players on the college campus. Thus, while you should take a solid set of courses and fulfill requirements, only the top schools emphasize completing a challenging curriculum, high grades, and standardized test scores.

FOR HIGHLY SELECTIVE COLLEGES, TALENT IS JUST THE BEGINNING

A few highly selective colleges seek extraordinary talent over academics, but most zero in on a student's challenging courses and high grades. To gain admission into the most highly selective colleges, you must take the most challenging course load you can manage and succeed. Highly selective colleges want disciplined scholars AND remarkably talented students.

Determine what you can handle, knowing that some colleges with extremely competitive admission will only take students who have completed more than ten AP, IB, or honors classes over the four years, including AP Calculus. AP Statistics is not of equal rigor in their eyes. Why, then, would these most competitive colleges require a class that is beyond the scope of what you need for your major? This situation is the $50,000 question. However, if taking AP calculus seems daunting, remember that most colleges that accept students for artistic fields do not require these types of classes.

College admissions can feel like a rollercoaster of energy and emotion. Creating a portfolio of talent, training, and experience is just the beginning. Meanwhile, some colleges want to see standardized test scores which are aided by practice. Applications and essays may seem easy at first, but managing the various requirements and deadlines can be difficult. Therefore, this application period is a good time to get a calendar and organize your tasks.

STANDARDIZED TESTING

A few schools require testing. Check first. Many colleges are test optional. This means that you are not required to take the SAT or ACT. However, if you do have a good score, it may make all the difference in accepting you. College admissions offices are studying this topic and considering their future policies. Much of their concern began with cancelations worldwide due to the pandemic. Schools did not want to let students into their site to take a standardized test who may be infected. In addition, social distancing limited the number of students who could take a test at a site at a time.

College admissions decisions were once centered around grades and test scores. The removal of the ACT/SAT requirement is significant at some colleges and has rattled admissions departments. Meanwhile, colleges proclaim that test-optional truly means that the test is not required, but evidence proves otherwise.

Thus, many students are still taking the test and working around the hurdles amid all of the confusion. Finally, competition continues to drive students to present evidence to show that they are worthy candidates.

In the end, colleges need to make a decision between very good candidates. If one student has a high score, that student may have a higher likelihood of admission depending upon the admissions committee's decision-making process. Data show that students who submitted scores within the college's range or higher were accepted at a higher rate than those without a score.

Some schools are test blind in that they say that they do not consider your scores. A few of these colleges still provide a place for you to input your scores. Thus, they are not truly blind. Nevertheless, this decision is yours. If the school does not require an admissions test, then you can choose to take the test. If your academics are solid and you are willing to prepare, you should take the test.

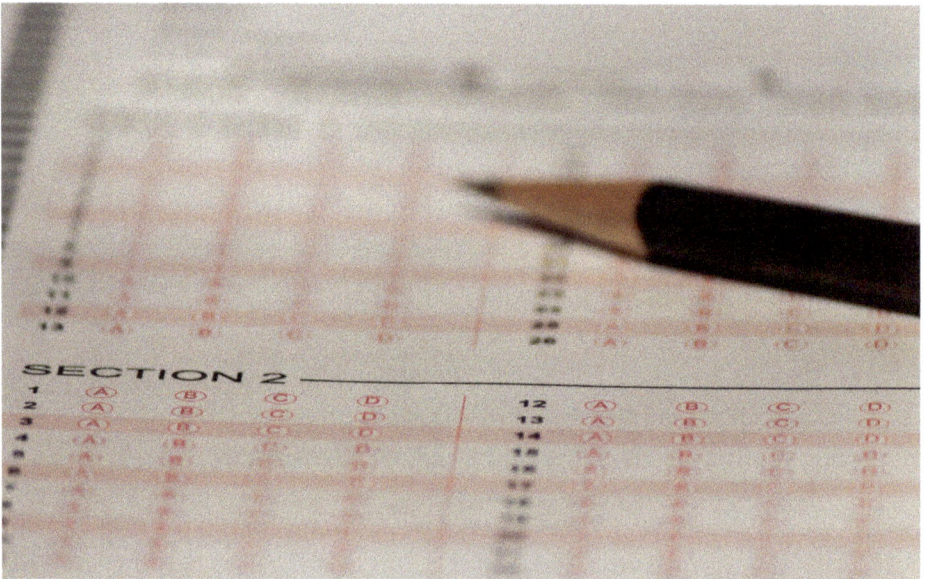

APPLYING EARLY

Early Action (EA), Restricted Early Action (REA), and Early Decision (ED)

With low acceptance rates, the chance to get more scholarship money, and chaos surrounding the cancellations and changes in AP, IB, SAT, and ACT testing, students clamor to apply early to schools. In addition, applications to top schools increased during the pandemic, resulting in colleges making difficult admissions decisions in their quest to build a diverse, talented, and engaged class of students.

Furthermore, students applying early have access to many more scholarship options. This confluence sent students in droves to apply early. This trend is likely to continue.

In Early Action (EA), Restricted Early Action (REA), and Early Decision (ED), students apply in late summer or early fall to college and generally find out around winter break, though some decisions come out earlier and a few arrive later. This advantage not only gives students the chance for more scholarship money in some cases but the benefit of finding out early reduces the tension during the long waiting period to find out about Regular Decision schools.

Early Action (EA) and Restricted Early Action (REA) are different. In Restricted Early Action, a limitation is placed on either how many or what colleges you can apply to simultaneously. Many REA schools do not allow students to apply to other Early Action schools, though some will allow students to apply EA to public colleges. In addition, some schools like Georgetown will allow students to apply EA elsewhere but not apply to a binding Early Decision (ED) program where the student commits to attending if they are accepted. However, most EA schools do not have these restrictions, and some students apply to a handful of EA schools during the admissions process.

Early Decision (ED) is a binding agreement between the student and college with signatures from the student's parents and the high school. Each of these parties acknowledges and agrees that, if granted admission, the student will attend. There are incentives. Frequently, acceptance rates are higher with ED. Also, at some schools, a large percentage of their class is filled with students who profess their unequivocal love for their dream school. Students who know they have a top choice school, have the necessary admissions requirements, and are committed to accepting the binding agreement to attend, should apply ED.

64

COMMON APPLICATION, COALITION APPLICATION, OR COLLEGE-SPECIFIC APPLICATION

Every college's process is unique. However, there are a few commonalities. In 2022, approximately 900 colleges used the Common App; about 150 colleges used the Coalition Application. A few used both. The University of California system has its own application as do the California State Universities and the Texas schools.

The Common App and Coalition App may be started early. In your junior year, consider getting a head start on reviewing what is required. The college-specific questions may change each year. However, the basic application is generally the same and can be created ahead of time. At the end of July, make a copy of everything you have completed just in case.

In August, most admissions applications are open and ready for you to dive into the college-specific questions. Some schools admit on a rolling basis. 'Rolling' means that periodically, after all of the materials are received, the admissions committee determines who they will accept, and they send the notification right away. Many students are accepted as early as August. The thrill of acceptance cannot be overstated.

Complete the application fully. Think carefully about optional sections. Typically, they offer you the chance to provide the school with just the right cherry on top of the ice cream sundae. If you have absolutely nothing to say, then leave it blank. There are often required essays on the main Common App and the supplemental applications for each school. Some include scholarship essays. Start early.

ADMISSIONS ESSAYS

For many people, writing is not an easy process. For students applying to college, personal statements and supplemental essays can be challenging. While much is at stake with your essays, essays are your friend. They can explain why you have a low grade or did not continue taking a class you started.

Everyone has a story to tell. In fact, life is an endless set of stories. With every passing moment new senses, thoughts, and experiences flood our stream of consciousness. We, in turn, tell these stories of life events to our family, friends, neighbors, and acquaintances. These stories provide definition to our life.

Relax and step back from the project and think about the highlights of your life. Now, which of those makes you a good student and worthy candidate?

Dedication? Persistence? Writing ability? Creative projects? Resilience in the face of fear? Love and compassion for family and friends? A talent in rock climbing, sailing, spelunking? Or maybe a service project where you helped save whales, rescued cats, or cleaned plastic bottles from the ocean?

Students ask me, "How can I give the essence of my entire life story in 650 words?" You can. First, decide what you want the college to know about you. What is the major point you want to make? Then, what stories do you have that exemplify those qualities you want to highlight? Afterwards, make an outline.

Even the short answers can be daunting but fun. Enjoy the process. While some essays are harrowing, others are fun. However, the starting point for a great college entrance essay is putting your pen to the paper. Pour out a conscious stream of thoughts. You can edit these later.

DECISIONS, DECISIONS: WAITING FOR A RESPONSE

The period between submitting your application and getting your results may not require a tremendous amount of work, but it does require patience and diligence. First, most schools will send you a link to a portal where you will check your results, though the most important reason for checking every couple of weeks is to ensure that they are not missing something or have not offered you the chance to apply for an extra scholarship. Check your portal regularly. Additionally, read the correspondence that the school may send through your e-mail.

Waiting is difficult. This is a tough period because students want to know. However, on the portal, the college typically lists the date they will send out the results. You will find out soon.

CELEBRATING ACCEPTANCES AND DEALING WITH REJECTION

Acceptance is not guaranteed. The probabilities are low at the most highly selective schools. However, you just need to work to have what it takes and give this commitment all you have.

Costume Design & Technical Theatre - Top 10 Most Competitive Schools by Admit Rate

1. Northwestern University - 9%
2. Tulane University - 11%
3. University of California, Los Angeles (UCLA) - 14%
4. University of Southern California (USC) - 16%
5. Carnegie Mellon University - 17%
6. Boston University - 20%

7. University of Michigan - 26%
8. California Institute of the Arts (CalArts) - 27%
9. Skidmore College - 32%
10. University of North Carolina School of the Arts - 36%

When you find out the results, celebrate your acceptances. Congratulations! These college admissions decisions go on your list of wins. Check your financial aid and scholarship package. Money is often an important factor in making your decision. Consider visiting the school. Many students apply by only looking at pictures and profiles on a website or book. There is nothing that replaces the actual visit. After all, you will be spending a few years there.

However, you may not be accepted everywhere you apply. The pandemic's uncertainty added more question marks to an already complicated set of admissions processes.

The 2020 buzzword was resilience. It is never easy to be rejected. However, rejection happens, and you will survive this. Note that many colleges still accept applications in April, May, and June. Look up those colleges. If you did not get accepted, you might want to see what other schools might be good options for you. You may be surprised to see the colleges on the list.

WAITLISTS: THE ART OF WAITING

Confirm immediately if you are given a waitlist spot and still want to attend. There is often a deadline, and you do not want to miss this. If you are no longer interested or have selected another school, go into the portal and turn down the offer. Someone else is bound to be thrilled by your anonymous gift.

Next, if you are highly interested, find the location on the portal or site designated by the college to update them on what you have done – accomplishments, awards, extra class, honors, art, shows, or films. You only want to add what they have not yet seen, but if you have taken the initiative to do something more than what you originally stated on the application, by all means, tell them. You could just wait for their decision, but you are better off being proactive and showing that you really want to be at their school.

Students do get off of the waitlists at most schools. Meanwhile, you will have to deposit somewhere else before the May 1st deadline. Stay hopeful. This next year will be a significant step along your journey. Relax!

DETERMINING FINANCIAL AID

You do not need to complete the FAFSA (Free Application for Federal Student Aid) or CSS Profile (College Scholarship Service) if you do not need aid. However, a handful of schools want to see one or both of these forms to obtain scholarships. Check now since there are deadlines.

If you completed the FAFSA (and CSS profile, if required), the financial aid package you receive would be viewable on your portal. The college will delineate the amounts you will receive for grants, loans, and work-study. Some students turn down work-study, but I caution against that. There are jobs on campus where you conduct research, work with a professor, work in the library, or assist an athletic team. Some of these jobs pay well, and you might have even done them as a volunteer.

Finally, if your financial situation changed since applied, you may be able to renegotiate the amount they offered.

CHOOSING THE RIGHT SCHOOL FOR YOU

Once you have acceptances, you need to make a decision. With the turmoil of the pandemic, disruption in clubs, sports, and experiential activities, and serious family health concerns, access to some opportunities has been non-existent. Most training and practice have been virtual. Furthermore, few students have traveled to visit colleges due to the crisis. However, with college costs for four years around $300,000 at some schools, college is the most significant investment some families will ever make. Furthermore, student loans can saddle a student in debt for a decade or more.

Financial decisions are key. However, there are many variables in deciding which school to choose. Will I be able to afford my education? Will classes be online or in-person? Will I be able to continue my training? Will I get to visit the colleges first? Can I mentally survive the repercussions of stressful decision-making? Should I defer my admissions and take a year off?

Once you make your decision, focus on your future. What is trending? What do people want? How can you deliver?

You've Got This!

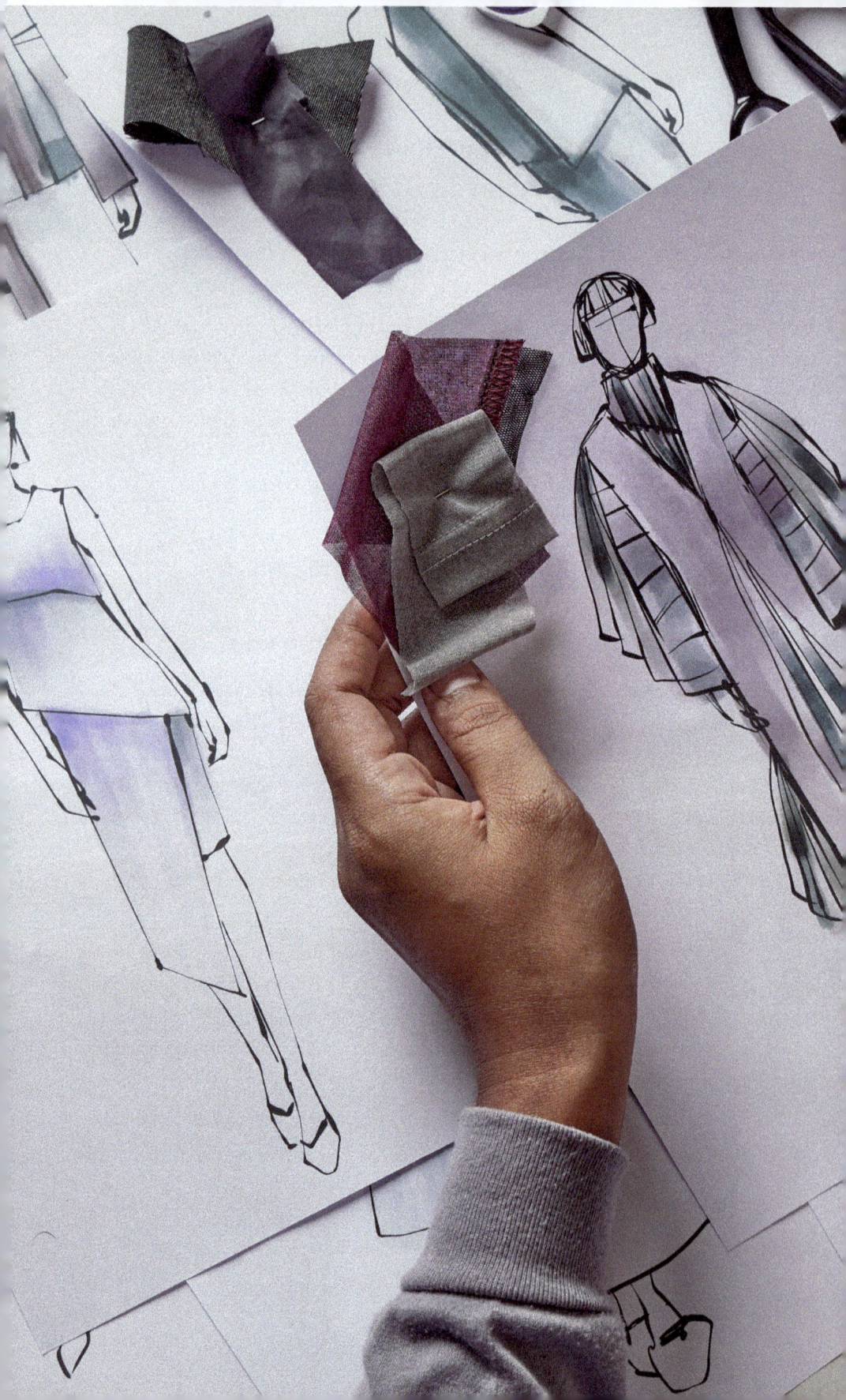

CHAPTER 10

PORTFOLIOS: REQUIREMENTS, ACCESS, AND PREPARATION

"The clown has great importance as part of the search for what is laughable and ridiculous in man. We should put the emphasis on the rediscovery of our own individual clown, the one that has grown up within us and which society does not allow us to express."

— **Jacques Lecoq**

THEATRE IS A TEAM SPORT

Theatre students must work together synchronously. Students do not register and take classes independently and study in their dorms. Students practice, train, learn new skills, and evolve with the ever-changing forces of theatre. New team members are invited to join after an audition, portfolio, and/or interview. Most of all, faculty leaders want to know if you will work well on their team and blend in with the talent they have.

Collaboration, sense of humor, disciplined work habits, willingness to exceed the call of duty, and a positive attitude are some of the essential ingredients to success in this field and behind the scenes. Also, theatre faculty members want to get to know you, determine your level of previous training, what you bring to the table, and how your skills can contribute to their productions. Theatre department directors are not ordinarily interested in training you from scratch and accepting you just because you are curious about theatre. They commit to working with you. You must be committed as well. Completely committed.

Theatre requires long hours, practically all-nighters, and balance with academics. You will still have classes while you are working on a show. Experience in high school or summer lets the school know that you can handle the rigors of theatre with the rigors of school, managing both successfully. This is also why the college wants you to submit recommendations, particularly from a theatre director or stage director who can vouch for your capabilities.

While some schools will not interview or require a creative design or technical theatre portfolio, you should be prepared to have samples of your work in pictures, video, website, drawings, recommendations, and written format, like an essay about your personal journey.

INTERVIEWS, AUDITIONS, AND PORTFOLIO REVIEWS

Interviews, auditions, and portfolio review days were once in person. Theatre admissions professionals sought to capture a person's body language, interaction with other people, and personality. In an audition, department members could create a stage and watch students perform as they might in a theatre. For acting, there was not only greater ability to evaluate singing and dance talent but they could watch multiple candidates at the same time and compare them side by side. This worked well as a few dozen applicants often auditioned on key dates, sometimes in locations around the country for convenience. Moreover, the process could be streamlined as well.

Furthermore, role-playing was easier in-person, giving theatre directors a sense of what the student might be like in collaborative situations. Interviews, auditions, and portfolio reviews also allowed students to network with people from the university and interact with potential future classmates. Additionally, when the audition or interview was on college campuses, students had the chance to visit the school, tour the facilities, gain a sense of what life might be like, learn about the program from the inside, meet people from other programs, and visit the dormitories.

PANDEMIC CHANGES

Yet, the pandemic demanded changes. With students unable to travel and colleges unable to allow students to visit the facilities, theatre departments adapted their auditions and interviews. Although many colleges were reticent, a few colleges took steps to offer online meetings, invitations to sit in on classes, and even in-person interviews. Still, with very few other choices, colleges moved their whole interview process online. Zoom, a platform that was virtually non-existent before the pandemic, rose in prominence as the pre-eminent method. As this new modus operandum took hold and more students, faculty, and admissions officers became comfortable, the rollout began.

Pre-screening with videos, film, pictures, resumes, drawings, designs, displays, and websites was fairly common before the pandemic. Application portfolios allowed students to input specified elements to a portal, and colleges began the evaluation process before determining who they would invite to their campus or centralized site. Scouts and recruiters also looked for talent at schools. However, with shows closed at most schools and summer programs canceled, there were few avenues to locate students for their program.

COSTS AND THEATRE PROGRAM VIABILITY

Frankly, even entire theatre programs were threatened at some colleges. Why maintain a theatre and associated staff if the college could not produce shows or most of the shows were canceled for nearly two years? With no costuming or facilities to work in, how would students learn the skills they need? With an uncertain future, the cost of traveling to recruit, audition, and secure student spots in a program that may no longer exist was called into question. Student costs were also a big factor in some of the decisions.

Without the cost to travel to interviews and evaluate auditoners online, theatre departments could invite more members of the community to participate in prospective applicants' online auditions. Any theatre faculty member, stage manager, behind-the-scenes director, or admissions staff member could attend by logging on and being part of the process.

The precariousness of life, concerns about health, and parents whose careers were in jeopardy were significant factors in the changes that took place. Families worried. Hunkered down in lockdowns, mandates, vaccine requirements, and illness, colleges needed creative options. After all, where should creativity begin?

ACCESS AND EQUITY

The other major factor was the costs involved. Many families could not afford to travel for interviews and auditions, particularly those students traveling from abroad. With the growing concern for access and equity, colleges worked harder to make the process fair for all applicants. The 2020 spotlight of BLM and issues surrounding diversity, racial and social inequity took center stage.

Colleges looked for new ways to level the playing field for all applicants.

By holding auditions on Zoom, Skype, Google Hangouts, Microsoft Teams, or Adobe Connect, students just needed a computer and an Internet connection. Quarantined or locked down, they could meet virtually from their home, school, or convenient location.

With a location in which the student was comfortable and without the financial burden of travel for themselves and often parents, students had greater access. For many students of color, auditions, interviews, or in-person portfolio reviews were significant barriers to entry. Removing these barriers became a central priority along with letting students know that everyone would have the chance to audition, interview, or be reviewed if they passed the initial portfolio evaluation process. Opportunity and access became the mantra of admissions offices nationwide.

Colleges sought new ways of putting together a diverse class. Creatively and thoughtfully, the playing field slowly leveled. There is more to do regarding access and equity, but steps were taken to allow more students and college representatives to be part of the process.

PORTFOLIOS

Portfolio requirement vary from school to school. More information is provided in the profiles in the second half of the book. Not all schools have portfolios, and not all schools have interviews. However, for schools requiring a portfolio, components often include a headshot or picture, resume, letters of recommendation, essays, theatre renderings, sketches, and artistic style. The following is only one example but offers a glimpse into the admissions process for technical theatre.

For example, for 2022 admissions, Boston University mentions the following:
- Interviews required
- Submit via Acceptd
- 20 files required
  - Headshot
  - Resume
  - Design & Production
    - Theatre renderings, painting or graphics, working drawings, ground plans, lighting plots, props, masks, etc.
  - Stage Management

- - Prompt books, programs, creative writing, director's notes
- Optional supplement:
    - o Recommendation letter
    - o 300-500 word prompt

Follow the instructions on the application and/or website to submit your portfolio. Portfolios are submitted in a specific way for each college. Read each website to determine the college's particular requirements. Some use SlideRoom, while others use Acceptd or iFolio, and still others require preliminary materials to be submitted through the basic application or directly to the college.

SLIDEROOM

SlideRoom partnered with the CommonApp to integrate the portfolio into their admissions process. Not all schools use SlideRoom, but it is a popular platform. Students check a box on the supplemental form of the CommonApp, and a portfolio link appears. Colleges receive the application while also gaining access to the portfolio from SlideRoom. When they import and view the student's data, they can evaluate each candidate based upon college requirements during that admissions cycle. Search features and image clarity make SlideRoom one of the most common platforms.

ACCEPTD

Acceptd is a popular platform for portfolios. Videos, resumes, art, essays, and other materials may be submitted. Also, interviews can be scheduled through this site in one seamless process. Acceptd is used by many colleges for its versatility.

IFOLIO

iFolio is a more recent addition to the college admissions scene. This modern digital platform offers an interactive portfolio. While iFolio is used more often for business interactions, interviews, and information sharing, some colleges find this tool extremely beneficial.

YOU'VE GOT THIS!

Whatever format a college requires, students upload their materials to provide a more seamless process for colleges to evaluate candidates for their programs. The portfolio process may seem cumbersome, particularly if you are applying to five to ten colleges with four to five different methods of submission and four to five different sets of requirements. However, if you start early and are disciplined in the process, you can do it. Even if you start late, you can pull everything together. It's just a bit more stressful. Get started now and prepare for your future.

BOLD NETWORKING

Networking takes social skills and a bit of moxie. From elevator speeches and restaurant encounters to tradeshows and industry meetings, your job is to find a way to get in front of people. How can you be recognized? Meet people and hand out your resume. Give them your business card and ask for their business card. Then, follow up and ask if you can call or meet them for lunch or coffee, even if asking may seem uncomfortable. Stay in touch with the people you meet, even if you just meet them out of happenstance or serendipity. Keep a log with each person's phone, e-mail, identifying information, and both date and location where you met. You never know when you will need it.

STAY IN TOUCH

Be proactive but professional. There is a delicate balance between keeping in touch and obsessively contacting an individual. Since each minute is critical to busy decision-makers, constant communication can overwhelm and frustrate the person you are attempting to impress or influence. Staying in touch every couple of months is fine. However, communicating more frequently can be overpowering. Remember that life is long. In the fashion industry, the network you grow will be valuable throughout your career.

Befriend other go-getters. They may be tremendous allies in the future, even if you are presently seeking the same position. Fellow interns today are likely to be very successful and hold prominent positions in the future. While staying in touch with "important" people may prove helpful now, remaining connected with your peers, particularly those who are bright and creative, may lead to mutually beneficial partnerships later. Thus, your contemporaries or peers are influential people...although not yet.

After interviewing at a few places, you may choose a position elsewhere. Even so, do not lose touch with the people you meet or burn bridges along the way.

This industry is not that big, and you will continually see movers and shakers on all levels of the fashion world. You never know. They may contact you to collaborate one day or meet for coffee at an event. Networking is a two-way street, and the best networkers know this.

COLLEGE AND CAREER CENTERS

Almost every college has a career center. There may be a specific career liaison in the fashion, fashion design, merchandising, business, or art department. Contact them for help in your search process. Not only can they assist with resume and cover letter services, but they may have contacts in the industry. Past graduates who are in the fashion industry make great connections. They have been through the ropes, they know a few people, and they might be able to get you an interview or into a fashion industry event. Any contact may be able to get your foot into the door.

LINKEDIN

LinkedIn is especially helpful for career searches. You can find numerous influential contacts on LinkedIn. After each interview, connect with them on LinkedIn. Keep a contact list of individuals you know in the fashion industry. Do not constantly try to connect with people you do not really know. However, if you have made the connection, occasionally keep in touch.

While some LinkedIn message boxes may be full and you may not get a reply, you can try. Occasionally, you hit on a lucky break. Though I do not have time to communicate with everyone, I have connected with some of my most inspiring authors, advisors, and intellectual leaders through LinkedIn.

FINALLY

Most people are willing to help you. Five percent will not. Thus, you have a 19 out of 20 chance of interacting with decent people who have the time and will give you advice. Don't lose faith in humanity just because you ran into a few people who are too busy to stop for you or are too self-absorbed that they cannot answer your question.

- Work ethic is everything.
- Excellence is expected.
- Learn what you do not know on your own time.
- Come to work prepared.
- Take constructive criticism well.
- Keep your cool under pressure.
- Avoid being timid.
- Stay on task.
- Come early.
- Stay late.
- Take your work seriously.
- Do more than expected.
- Read your e-mail/texts after hours in case something is important.
- Ask questions. No question is too stupid.
- Maintain a clean workspace.
- Dress and act professionally.
- Don't gossip or complain.
- Avoid frustrating your phenomenally busy supervisor.
- Be straightforward, and don't beat around the bush.

You've Got This!

CHAPTER 11

POST-PANDEMIC EMPLOYMENT OUTLOOK: STATISTICS AND ECONOMIC PROJECTIONS

"It's time to trust my instincts. Close my eyes. And Leap."

- Wicked

COSTUME DESIGN AND COSTUME ATTENDANTS

There are many more costume attendants than costume designers. Typically, a show will have one or two creatives who envision, draw, and produce the overall designs. Meanwhile, there are numerous individuals who sew, stitch, and craft the actual costumes and a few who serve as attendants to help with the fittings and wardrobe changes. Once a show is created, there are few overall design changes. The rest of the work is in the hands of the stitchers and attendants. The salary for costume attendants is not much more than minimum wage. According to the Bureau of Labor Statistics, the industry will grow 10.8% over the next decade. The mean annual wage is $51,780, though the median wage is $42,910.[1] This lower amount is because those in costume and wardrobe are paid more in New York City, where the cost of living is high and the pay is higher too. Everywhere else the pay is considerably lower.

According to the Bureau of Labor Statistics, the industries with the greatest demand for those in costume and wardrobe are:

1. Motion Picture and Video Industries
2. Performing Arts Companies
3. Colleges, Universities, and Professional Schools
4. Traveler Accommodation
5. Promoters of Performing Arts, Sports, and Entertainment

MAKEUP ARTISTS, THEATRICAL AND PERFORMANCE

Shows of all kinds require technical experience in makeup. However, individuals are willing to pay for expert skills in design. The experience required to enter this field on a higher level is a key factor in the higher wage, though 25% earn lower than $65,000. Still, the industry is growing the pay is increasing.

According to the Bureau of Labor Statistics, the industry will grow 13.8% over the next decade. The mean annual wage is $99,990, though the median wage is $106,920.[2]

According to the Bureau of Labor Statistics, the industries with the greatest demand for makeup artists are:

1. Motion Picture and Video Industries

---

1 U.S. Bureau of Labor Statistics, "Occupational Employment and Wages, May 2020 – 39-3092 Costume Attendants," *U.S. Bureau of Labor Statistics,* May 2020, https://www.bls.gov/oes/current/oes393092.htm
2 Ibid.

2. Personal Care Services
3. Performing Arts Companies
4. Employment Services

SET AND EXHIBIT DESIGNERS

Designing sets is essential for theatre, films, and even corporations. The skills are transferrable to conference presentations, shows, window dressings, and other presentations. Set and exhibit designers create the visual impression for an audience in film, video, television, and theatre. Set and exhibit designers not only have the artistic and technical background, but also use their creativity to incorporate scripts, visual cues, and ideas from others involved. Many conduct research on period details and architectural styles.

According to the Bureau of Labor Statistics, the industry will grow 9.6% over the next decade. The mean annual wage is $64,610, though the median wage is $58,180.[3] This lower amount is because the pay is higher in New York City, where the cost of living is high and the pay is higher too. Elsewhere the pay is considerably lower.

3 U.S. Bureau of Labor Statistics, "Occupational Employment and Wages, May 2020 – 27-1027 Set and Exhibit Designers," *U.S. Bureau of Labor Statistics*, May 2020, https://www.bls.gov/oes/current/oes271027.htm

According to the Bureau of Labor Statistics, the industries with the greatest demand for set and exhibit designers are:

1. Motion Picture and Video Industries
2. Performing Arts Companies
3. Museums, Historical Sites, and Similar Institutions
4. Independent Artists, Writers, and Performers
5. Colleges, Universities, and Professional Schools

BROADCAST, SOUND, AND VIDEO TECHNICIANS

While some in the audio industry work in theatre, most of the positions are in radio, television, movie, and recording studios. They often hold positions in hotels, arenas, offices, and schools. Most people in this field learn on the job, but many have a college or professional school education. The educational requirements vary by the job.

According to the Bureau of Labor Statistics, the industry will grow 21% over the next decade, which is significantly higher than the national average for other careers. The median annual wage is $50,000.[4] There were 138,700 people employed in this field in 2020.

4   U.S. Bureau of Labor Statistics, "Occupational Outlook Handbook – Broadcast, Sound, and Video Technicians," *U.S. Bureau of Labor Statistics*, n.d., https://www.bls.gov/ooh/media-and-communication/broadcast-and-sound-engineering-technicians.htm

ACTORS

Actors are needed both on stage as well as in numerous other fields. While some actors work in theatre, most of the positions are in film, television, and media. Most people in this field learn on the job. Many also have a college or professional acting school education. However, actors continually train to keep up their skills.

According to the Bureau of Labor Statistics, the industry will grow 32% over the next decade, which is significantly higher than the national average for other careers. This is partly because many companies employ actors as representatives or to create videos for promotions and re-enactments. The median annual wage is $21.88 per hour.[5] The reason for the hourly wage rather than a yearly wage is that most actors are hired for short-term projects with roles lasting from one day to a couple of months. There were 51,600 people employed in this field in 2020.

PRODUCERS AND DIRECTORS

Producers and directors typically work in theatre or film, creating motion pictures, television programming, live theatre, commercials, and other productions. Producers and directors earn a bachelor's degree, though many have a graduate degree. While most knowledge is learned on the job, a business background is valuable along with a film/theatre education. Educational skills vary by the job.

With time and budgetary pressures, this position can be stressful. Work hours are often long and unpredictable.

According to the Bureau of Labor Statistics, the industry will grow 24% over the next decade, which is significantly higher than the national average for other careers. The median annual wage is $76,400.[6] There were 131,000 people employed in this field in 2020.

5   U.S. Bureau of Labor Statistics, "Occupational Outlook Handbook – Actors," *U.S. Bureau of Labor Statistics*, n.d., https://www.bls.gov/ooh/entertainment-and-sports/actors.htm

6   U.S. Bureau of Labor Statistics, "Occupational Outlook Handbook – Producers and Directors," *U.S. Bureau of Labor Statistics*, n.d., https://www.bls.gov/ooh/entertainment-and-sports/producers-and-directors.htm

CHAPTER 12

NEXT STEPS: CAREER OPTIONS, PREPARATION, AND CREATING WONDER BACKSTAGE

"Close your eyes and let the music set you free."

– Phantom of the Opera

VERSATILITY IS A MUST

There are numerous avenues to pursue in theatre. Costume design and technical theatre are just two with multiple skill sets. Contained within each of these broad areas, cross-training is a virtue and probably a must. Designing a costume, creating a wig, and applying makeup may be required as an apprentice in costume design. In a similar way, painting, construction, carpentry, lighting, and sound, while extremely diverse talents may be essential. If "the show must go on", an "expert" with a BFA in technical theatre typically has the skillset to perform a wide range of tasks. The more areas you can manage, the greater your versatility, and the better the chance you have of landing the position you want.

CREATING WONDER BACKSTAGE

Few people know what really happens backstage. Some do not want to know. Others believe that it would spoil the magic to learn the nuances of the special effects. However, the magic happens when the lights go down and the action behind the scenes begins. Although often thankless and unseen, the work of costume designers and theatre technicians is phenomenal and essential. This book is an acknowledgement of the hard work that happens when teams put aside differences, gel as a unit, and get to work day in and day out to bring the theatre to life.

CAREER OPTIONS

The following summer positions and job descriptions came from the Texas Shakespeare Festival.[1] While there may be additional career options like directing and managing, these positions directly align with the degrees discussed in this book.

COSTUME DEPARTMENT

Costume Director/Head of Wardrobe

Minimum requirements: two years of professional experience in a supervisory capacity required.

May 18 arrive / August 3 depart
$5,000 / up to $300 travel / private dorm housing / 14 meals a week

Costume Department Director is responsible for:

---

1   Texas Shakespeare Festival, "Costume Department," T*exas Shakespeare Festival*, n.d., https://www.texasshakespeare.com/costumes

- Creating daily schedule of the costume shop operations
- Determining the viability of proposed designs regarding budget, time, and labor
- Coordinating measurements and fittings
- Supervising cutter/drapers, first hands, stitchers, wardrobe personnel, and interns
- Maintaining adequate supplies and equipment
- Conducting shop meetings
- Attending production meetings
- Keeping track of budgets and processing receipts
- Assisting with any public relations or community outreach events such as fundraisers, Media Day, displays, interviews, informal talks, etc.
- Coordinating strike of all costume-related areas
- Participating in opening night discussions

Head of Wardrobe is responsible for:
- Setting up, organizing, and maintaining the racks and storage systems required for the productions
- Organizing and supervising costume load-in and load-out, costume changes, and quick chances for each production
- Cleaning and maintaining the dressing rooms and related areas
- Supervising dressers and making personnel assignments
- Cleaning and maintaining all costume items during the run of the show
- Assuming responsibility for all costumes and accessories in the productions after opening night
- Discussing with the Artistic Director any costume-related issue that could alter the visual design of a production after the show opens
- Participating in opening night discussions

Cutter/Drapers (2)

May 18 arrive / July 5 depart
$4,000 / up to $300 travel / double occupancy dorm housing / 14 meals a week

Minimum requirement: preferred master's degree and/or two years of professional experience.

Responsible for:
- Developing patterns and cutting all fabric, including facings, linings, bias strips, plackets, etc.

- Working with the designers and the costume shop manager to plan the construction process for each garment
- Instructing and supervising first hands and stitchers
- Offering group tutorials to ensure consistent quality and efficiency
- Working within the parameters of budget and production schedule
- Assisting designers and shop manager to coordinate fitting schedules
- Attending fittings
- Supervising alterations
- Preparing swatch bags for each designer
- Cleaning cutting area and preparing all patterns and unused fabrics for restocking
- Participating in opening night discussions

Wig Stylist

May 20 arrive / July 5 depart
$3,500 / up to $300 travel / single occupancy dormitory suite / 14 meals a week

Minimum requirements: MFA in theatre preferred, or 3 years of professional experiences as Wig Master or Assistant Wig Master.

Desired skills include wig design, construction, fronting and ventilating, facial hair construction, wig maintenance, wig and hairstyling, and thorough knowledge of period of styles.

Responsible for:

- Constructing wigs, hairstyles, and facial hairpieces to meet costume designer's specifications
- Establishing priorities and working within budget, labor, and time constraints
- Purchasing and /or renting wig materials, supplies, and equipment
- Supervising the maintenance of all wigs and hairpieces for a four-show repertory

Duties include:

- Constructing or acquiring wigs and all hairpieces for four shows
- Instructing wardrobe crew members in the maintenance of wigs and all hairpieces
- Pulling wigs and hairpieces from current TSF stock, when possible
- Developing a budget based on designs

- Working within a tight budget and under severe deadlines
- Attending all meetings, rehearsals, and performances as needed

Assistant Wig Stylist

May 20 arrive / August 3 depart
$2,500 / up to $300 travel / double occupancy dormitory housing / 14 meals a week

Minimum requirements: BFA in theatre preferred, or one year of professional experience working on wigs and hairstyling.

Desired skills include construction, fronting and ventilating, facial hair construction, wig and hairstyling, and thorough knowledge of period hairstyles.

Responsible for:

- Assist with constructing wigs, hairstyles, and facial hairpieces to meet costume designer's specifications
- Washing and combing out wigs as needed
- Assist with maintaining a clean and safe working environment
- To maintain wigs and hairpieces during the performances
- Assist in company strike

First Hands (2)

May 20 arrive / July 5 depart
$3,000 / up to $300 travel / double occupancy dorm housing / 14 meals a week

Minimum requirements: MFA in theatre preferred and/or two year of professional experience.

Responsible for:

- Serving as the cutter/draper's assistant
- Working with the cutter/draper to supervise/instruct stitchers
- Helping to maintain the production schedule
- Re-threading sergers as needed
- Maintaining the industrial irons
- Performing all duties of a stitcher
- Participating in opening night discussions

Stitcher / Wardrobe Crew (5)

May 20 arrive / August 3 depart
$3,000 / up to $300 travel / double occupancy dorm housing / 14 meals a week

Minimum requirements: BFA in theatre preferred and/or one year of professional experience

Stitcher is responsible for:

- Assembling garments as instructed by the cutter/drapers and first hands
- Machine sewing and all hand finishing, closures, hems, etc.
- Assisting with crafts and other related tasks as required
- Maintains assigned sewing machine and work area
- Assisting with company strike
- Participating in opening night discussions

Wardrobe is responsible for:

- Assuming duties as "Head of Wardrobe" for a particular show, assuming the responsibilities associated with that position
- Assisting the Head of Wardrobe in preparing and maintaining the costumes for each production
- Assisting with costume check-in/check-out, and changeover
- Assisting actors with getting dressed for each production

- Executing quick changes as assigned by the Head of Wardrobe
- Assisting with company strike
- Participating in opening night discussions

Costume Intern / Wardrobe

May 20 arrive / August 3 depart
$1,500 / double occupancy dorm housing / 14 meals a week

Minimum requirements: undergraduate costume technology training required and/or one year of professional experience

Note: Costume Interns are assigned primarily to the costume department, but may also be reassigned, as needed, to other technical areas.

Responsible for:
- Working as a stitcher/wardrobe for all productions
- Assisting the Costume Shop Manager in cleaning and maintaining costume storage
- Participating in opening night discussions
- Assisting with company strike

Costume and Wig Stylist Intern

May 20 arrive / August 3 depart
$1,500 / double occupancy dormitory housing / 14 meals a week

Minimum requirements: undergraduate training in wigs and hairstyling preferred and/or one year of professional experience working on wigs and hairstyling.

Desired skills include construction, fronting and ventilating, facial hair construction, wig and hairstyling.

Responsible for:
- Assist with constructing wigs, hairstyles, and facial hairpieces to meet costume designer's specifications
- Washing and combing out wigs as needed
- Assist with maintaining a clean and safe working environment
- To maintain wigs and hairpieces during the performances
- Serve as wardrobe crew as needed and assist with full company strike

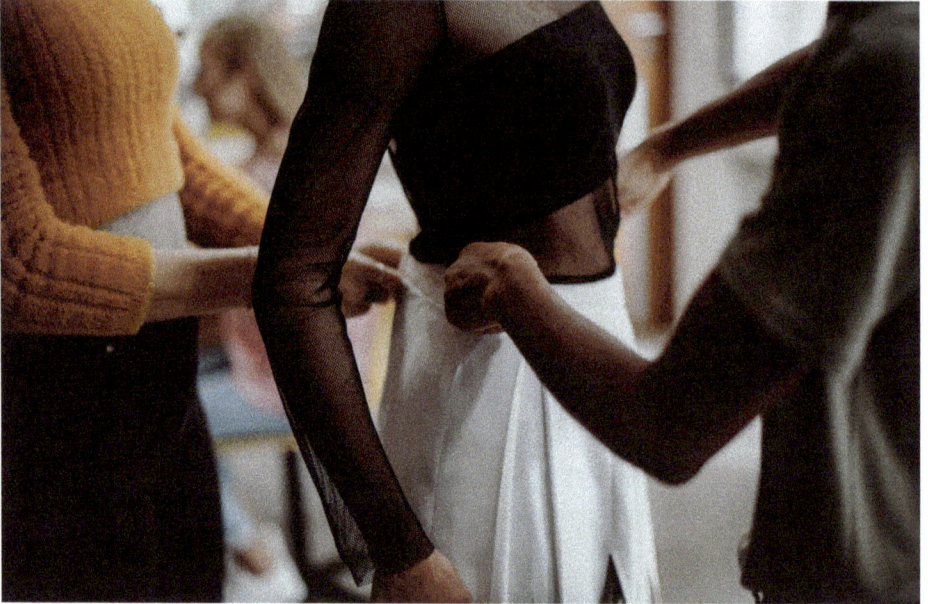

DESIGNERS

Scenic Designer

May 16 arrive / July 5 depart
$6,000 stipend / up to $400 travel / private dorm housing / 14 meals a week

Minimum requirement: preferred Master's degree and/or three years of professional design experience

Responsible for:

- Designing all scenic elements for a four-show rotating repertory season
- Working with the properties designer in the implementation of all properties
- Supplying all drawings and models or renderings for the four designs
- Working within the allotted budget and production schedule
- Participating in opening night discussions

Costume Designers (2)

May 16 arrive / July 5 depart
$5,500 stipend / up to $400 travel / private dorm housing with private bath / 14 meals a week

Minimum requirement: Master's degree completed by May 2020 and three years of professional design experience

Responsible for:

- Designing all costumes, accessories, hairstyles, and specialty makeup for two of the four repertory shows
- Providing color renderings for possible exhibition
- Working within the allotted budget and production schedule
- Purchasing all fabrics, trims, and accessories in coordination with the Costume Shop Manager
- Accounting for all expenditures
- Consulting with the cutters/drapers about patterns and construction methods
- Attending first read-throughs, fittings, production meetings, and dress rehearsals
- Serving as the primary craftsperson, dyer, milliner, and wig stylist on their two productions
- Generating all show-related paperwork, including actor/scene charts, dressing lists, quick-change lists, etc.
- Attending, when requested, public relations events: media day, post-show discussions, interviews, and presentations
- Participating in opening night discussions

Lighting Designer

May 20 arrive / July 5 depart
$6,000 stipend / up to $400 travel / private dorm housing / 14 meals a week

Minimum requirement: preferred Master's degree and/or three years of professional design experience

Responsible for:

- Designing, creating, and documenting all lighting effects for the main four-show repertory
- Supervising all personnel and work within the lighting department
- Working within the allotted budget and production schedule
- Accounting for all expenditures
- Attending, when requested, public relations events: media day, post-show discussions, interviews, and presentations
- Participating in opening night discussions

Sound Designer

May 20 arrive / July 5 depart

$5,000 stipend / up to $400 travel / private dorm housing / 14 meals a week

Minimum requirement: preferred Master's degree and/or three years of professional design experience

Responsible for:

- Designing, creating, and acquiring all sound effects and music for the main four-show repertory
- Supervising all personnel and work within the sound department
- Working within the allotted budget and production schedule
- Accounting for all expenditures
- Implementing and documenting the festival sound and video system set-up
- Attending, when requested, public relations events: media day, post-show discussions, interviews, and presentations
- Participating in opening night discussions

PROPERTIES DEPARTMENT

Properties Master

May 16 arrive / August 3 depart
$4,000 stipend / up to $300 travel / single occupancy dorm housing / 14 meals a week

Minimum Requirements: Advanced skills in management, scheduling, bookkeeping, and budgeting. Proficient in woodworking and painting. Knowledge of molding & casting and finishing techniques. General knowledge of period style. The ideal candidate should be self-motivated, safety conscious, and a team player with at least two years of professional experience in properties management, or equivalent combination of education and experience.

Responsible for:

- Communicate with stage managers and directors to maintain a consistently up to date properties list and rehearsal properties needs
- Issue call times and coordinate crew member schedules around changeoover and run crew responsibilities
- Oversee the department's budget, including any purchases made in stores or online and turning in receipts and purchasing sheets
- Maintain organization of tools in the shop and properties in stock storage
- Assist with the construction and/or acquistion of properties for the children's production and other auxiliary shows

- Performing all duties within the parameters of the allotted budget and production schedule
- Assisting with company strike
- Participate in opening night discussions

Assistant Properties Master

May 16 arrive / August 3 depart
$3,000 stipend / up to $300 travel / double occupancy dorm housing / 14 meals a week

Minimum Requirements: Proficient in woodworking and painting. Knowledge of molding & casting and finishing techniques. General knowledge of period style. The ideal candidate should be self-motivated, safety conscious, and a team player with at least two years of professional experience in properties management, or equivalent combination of education and experience.

Responsible for:

- Assisting the properties master in all areas, including any purchases made in stores or online and turning in receipts and purchasing sheets
- Maintain organization of tools in the shop and properties in stock storage
- Assist with the construction and/or acquistion of properties for the children's production and other auxiliary shows
- Performing all duties within the parameters of the allotted budget and production schedule
- Assisting with company strike
- Participate in opening night discussions

Properties Artisan

May 20 arrive / August 3 depart
$2,500 stipend / up to $300 travel / double occupancy dorm housing / 14 meals a week

Minimum Requirements: Art experience and creative skills preferred. Advanced skills in woodworking and painting. Skills in molding & casting, paint finishing techniques, and paper projects. General knowledge of period style. The ideal candidate should be self-motivated, safety conscious, and a team player with at least one year of professional experience in properties and construction, or equivalent combination of education and experience.

Responsible for:

- Assisting in construction and/or acquisition of all properties for the four-

heights above 25'. Ideal candidate should have at least one year of professional experience, or equivalent combination of educational experience.

Responsible for:

- Assisting the Technical Director and Assistant Technical Director with materials inventory
- Building all scenic elements and set props for the four-show rotating repertory season, children's show, and auxiliary shows as needed with a focus on complicated or advanced scenic pieces
- Serving on the scenic running and change-over crews
- Participating in opening night discussions
- Assisting with company strike

Scenic Carpenters (5)

May 16 arrive /August 3 depart
$4,400 stipend / up to $300 / double occupancy dorm housing / 14 meals a week

Minimum Requirements: Experience with various scenic construction techniques and materials; strong woodworking skills; proficiency with time management; ability to routinely lift at least 50 pounds, spend extended periods of time on your feet, work a varied schedule, and to work at heights above 25'.

Responsible for:

- Building all scenic elements for the four-show rotating repertory season and children's show
- Serving on the scenic running and changeover crews
- Participating in opening night discussions
- Assisting with company strike

PAINT DEPARTMENT

Scenic Charge Artist

May 16 arrive / July 5 depart
$3,500 stipend / up to $300 travel / private dorm housing / 14 meals a week

Minimum Requirements: Experience in creating samples for approval by Scenic Designer, mixing color, paint mixing, and scenic treatments including, but not limited to, faux finish, carving, texturing, ageing, distressing, and general working ability in both latex and scenic paint. The candidate should also have experience in reading blueprints and color elevations, budget management, scheduling, and be comfortable working at heights above 16'. Ideal candidate should be self-motivated, safety conscious, with at least three years of professional experience, or equivalent combination of education and experience.

Responsible for:

- Maintaining paint stock, budget, and purchasing
- All the painting of scenic elements for the four-show rotating repertory season and a children's show
- Working closely with the Scenic Designer and Technical Director on all scenic painting projects
- Participating in opening night discussions
- Assisting with company strike

Assistant Charge Artist

May 16 arrive / August 3 depart
$3,500 stipend / up to $300 travel / double occupancy dorm housing / 14 meals a week

Minimum Requirements: Experience in scenic treatments including, but not limited to, faux finish, carving, texturing, aging, distressing, and general working ability in both latex and scenic paint. The candidate should also have experience in reading blueprints and color elevations and be comfortable working at heights above 16'. The ideal candidate should be self-motivated and safety conscious, with at least two years of professional experience, or equivalent combination of education and experience.

Responsible for:

- Assisting the Scenic Charge Artist on all painting duties for the four-show rotating repertory season
- Assisting the Scenic Charge Artist in maintaining paint stock and necessary departmental purchasing
- Assisting the Scenic Charge Artist in supervising the paint department
- Participating in opening night discussions
- Maintain paint treatments throughout changeovers
- Paint Charging the Children's Show
- Assist with company strike

Scenic Artist

May 16 arrive / July 5 depart
$1,800 stipend / up to $300 travel / double occupancy dorm housing / 14 meals a week

Minimum Requirements: Experience in scenic treatments including, but not limited to, faux finish, carving, texturing, aging, distressing, and general working ability in both latex and scenic paint. The candidate should also have some experience in reading blueprints and color elevations and be comfortable working at heights above 16'. The ideal candidate should be self-motivated and safety conscious, with at least one year of professional experience, or equivalent combination of education and experience.

Responsible for:

- Assisting the Scenic Charge and Assistant Scenic Charge with all painting duties for the four-show rotating repertory season, children's show, and auxiliary shows as needed
- Assist with intern training
- Participating in opening night discussions
- Assist in maintaining painted elements during the run of the shows
- Serve on the running crew and change-over crew

Scene Painting Intern (2)

May 20 arrive / August 3 depart
$1,500 stipend / double occupancy dorm housing / 14 meals a week

Minimum Requirements: Fundamental experience in scenic treatments including, but not limited to, faux finish, carving, texturing, aging, and distressing. The candidate should also be comfortable working at heights above 16'. The ideal candidate should be self-motivated and safety conscious with at least two years of college training in technical theatre, or equivalent combination of education and experience.

Note: Scene Painting Interns are assigned primarily to the painting department, but may also be reassigned, as needed, to other technical areas.

Responsible for:

- Assisting with all painting duties for the four-show rotating repertory season, children's show, and auxiliary shows as needed
- Serving on the properties running and change-over crews
- Assisting with company strike
- Participating in opening night discussions

LIGHTING DEPARTMENT

Master Electrician

May 20 arrive / August 3 depart
$4,000 stipend / up to $300 travel / private dorm housing / 14 meals a week

The Texas Shakespeare Festival is seeking a Master Electrician to join our team in Kilgore, Texas for the 2021 summer season. TSF is committed to creating a diverse and inclusive environment ensuring that all qualified applicants will receive equal consideration for employment. The successful candidate will possess solid leadership, communication, organizational skills; electrics team leadership and lighting design experience whether academically or professionally; experience with ETC Element console and ability to program efficiently and accurately; experience with programming and maintaining moving lights and LED fixtures, knowledge of theatrical rigging, electricity and wiring; ability to read and understand light plots and related lighting paperwork, and ability to lift at least 50 pounds and able to work from ladders and other heights.

Responsible for:

- Implementing the lighting design (installing, repairing, and maintaining all lighting equipment) for a four-show rotating repertory season, the children's show, and auxiliary shows as needed
- Construct and wire any scenic or practical items such as light boxes, LED Tape, or other production-specific lighting
- Maintain accurate and up to date paperwork for each production and changeover
- Keep electrics lab and booth areas clean and free of debris
- Follow all health and safety guidelines established by the theatre. Report any unsafe conditions or practices to your supervisor immediately
- Supervising and assigning electrics duties to running and change-over crews
- Serving as the light board operator for at least one show
- Serve as the deck electrician for at least one show
- Serving as the Lighting Designer for the children's show
- Assisting with company strike
- Participating in opening night discussions

Assistant Master Electrician

May 20 arrive / August 3 depart
$3,000 stipend / up to $300 travel / double occupancy dorm housing / 14 meals a week

Minimum Requirements: Assist Master Electrician in supervising a 4 member team of electricians through the installation, repair, and maintenance of all elements of the lighting design and changeovers. The successful candidate will have a minimum of one year of professional theatrical lighting experience or the educational equivalent with an emphasis in programming ETC Consoles. Also required is knowledge of industry standard operating procedures, and electrical theory and electrical safety.

Responsible for:

- Assisting with the implementation of the lighting design for the four-show rotating repertory season, the children's show, and other auxiliary shows, as needed
- Serving as the Master Electrician for the children's show
- Helping to install, repair, and maintain all lighting equipment
- Assisting with running and change-over crews
- Serving as the light board operator for at least one show
- Serving as deck electrician for at least one show
- Assisting with company strike
- Participating in opening night discussions
- Serve as Lighting Designer for the Chinese Show

Lighting Intern (2)

May 20 arrive / August 3 depart
$1,500 stipend / double occupancy dorm housing / 14 meals a week

Minimum Requirements: Assist with the hang, focus, and strike of electrics and special effects for all productions; Program and run the lighting console for shows as assigned; Assist with the maintenance and upkeep for all lighting inventory and systems. The successful candidate will have a minimum of one year of educational theatrical lighting experience.

Note: Lighting Interns are assigned primarily to the lighting department, but may also be reassigned, as needed, to other technical areas.

Responsible for:

- Assisting with the implementation of the lighting design for the four-show rotating repertory season, the children's show, and other auxiliary shows, as needed
- Helping to install and maintain all lighting equipment
- Working on the running and change-over crews in lighting

- Serving as the light board operator for at least two shows
- Assisting with company strike
- Participating in opening night discussions

STAGE MANAGEMENT

Stage Manager (2)

Each Stage Manager is assigned to two shows

Minimum requirement: preferred Master's degree and/or three years of professional stage management experience

May 18 arrive / August 3 depart
$4,000 stipend / up to $300 travel / private dorm housing / 14 meals a week

Responsible for:

- Stage managing two shows in a four-show rotating repertory season
- Organizing and implementing the daily rehearsal schedule
- Scheduling and posting rehearsal and production calls
- Compiling production books that become the property of the festival
- Calling from the control booth the two shows assigned
- Attending all scheduled rehearsals, paper techs, dry techs, technical rehearsals and performances
- Participating in opening night discussions
- Participating, if needed, in media day
- Performing other stage managing duties that are deemed necessary and appropriate

Assistant Stage Manager / Stage Manager Children's Show

May 18 arrive / August 3 depart
$2,500 stipend / up to $300 travel / double occupancy dorm housing / 14 meals a week

Minimum requirement: completed undergraduate degree and/or one year of professional stage management experience

Responsible for:

- Assisting the assigned Stage Manager with all duties on two shows in the four-show rotating repertory season
- Assisting with backstage running assignments for the crews
- Performing backstage duties during performances as assigned by the

Stage Manager

- Attending all scheduled rehearsals, paper techs, dry techs, technical rehearsals and performances
- Participating in the opening night discussions
- Serving as the stage manager for the children's show and the TSF Talent Show
- Performing other stage management duties that are deemed necessary and appropriate
- Assisting with company strike

Assistant Stage Manager / Stage Manager Talent Showcase

May 18 arrive / August 3 depart
$2,500 stipend / up to $300 / double occupancy dorm housing / 14 meals a week

Minimum requirement: completed undergraduate degree and/or one year of professional stage management experience

Responsible for:

- Assisting the assigned Stage Manager with all duties on two shows in the four-show rotating repertory season
- Assisting with backstage running assignments for the crews
- Performing backstage duties during performances as assigned by the Stage Manager
- Attending all scheduled rehearsals, paper techs, dry techs, technical rehearsals and performances
- Participating in the opening night discussions
- Serving as the stage manager for the Chinese Theatre Night
- Performing other stage management duties that are deemed necessary and appropriate
- Assisting with company strike

Stage Management Intern / Assistant Stage Manager for the Children's Show and Talent Show

May 20 arrive / August 3 depart
$1,500 stipend / double occupancy dorm housing / 14 meals a week

Minimum requirement: one year undergraduate stage management training

Responsible for:

- Assisting the assigned Stage Manager and Assistant Stage Manager with all duties on two shows in the four-show rotating repertory season

- Assisting with backstage running assignments for the crews
- Performing backstage duties during performances as assigned by the Stage Manager and Assistant Stage Manager
- Attending all scheduled rehearsals, paper techs, dry techs, technical rehearsals and performances
- Participating in the opening night discussions
- Serving as the Assistant Stage Manager for the children's show and Chinese Theatre Night
- Performing other stage management duties that are deemed necessary and appropriate
- Assisting with company strike

Stage Management Intern / Assistant Stage Manager for the Children's Show and TSF Talent Showcase

May 20 arrive /August 3 depart
$1,500 stipend / double occupancy dorm housing / 14 meals a week

Minimum requirement: minimum one year undergraduate stage management training

Responsible for:

- Assisting the assigned Stage Manager and Assistant Stage Manager with all duties on two shows in the four-show rotating repertory season
- Assisting with backstage running assignments for the crews
- Performing backstage duties during performances as assigned by the Stage Manager and Assistant Stage Manager
- Attending all scheduled rehearsals, paper techs, dry techs, technical rehearsals and performances
- Participating in the opening night discussions
- Serving as the Assistant Stage Manager for the children's show and the TSF Talent Showcase
- Performing other stage management duties that are deemed necessary and appropriate
- Assisting with company strike

4
Regions

57
Programs

COLLEGE PROFILES AND REQUIREMENTS

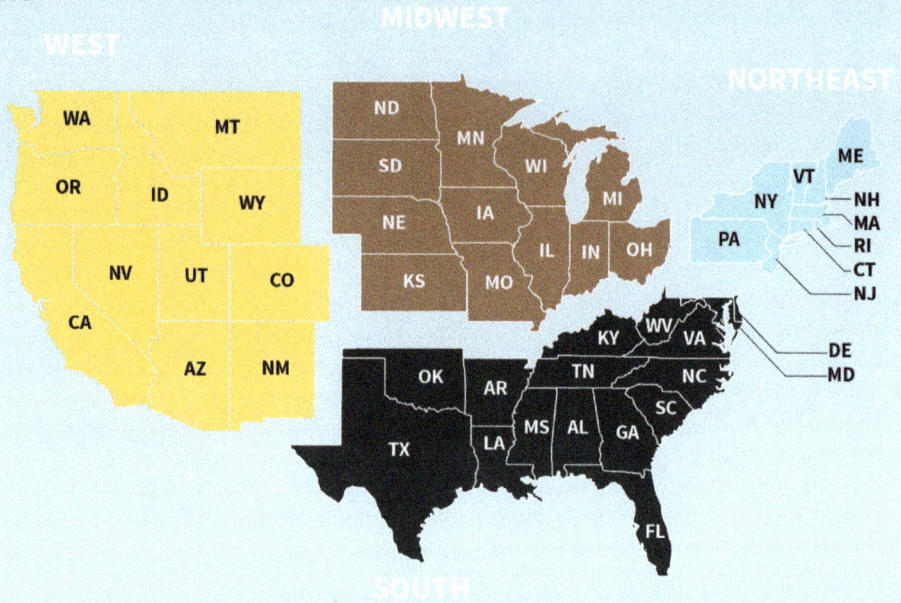

WEST
MIDWEST
NORTHEAST
SOUTH

PROGRAMS BY REGION
U.S. CENSUS BUREAU CLASSIFICATIONS

REGION 1 – NORTHEAST

Connecticut, Maine, Massachusetts, New Hampshire, New Jersey, New York, Pennsylvania, Rhode Island, and Vermont

REGION 2 – MIDWEST

Illinois, Indiana, Iowa, Kansas, Michigan, Minnesota, Missouri, Nebraska, North Dakota, Ohio, South Dakota, and Wisconsin

REGION 3 – SOUTH

Alabama, Arkansas, Delaware, District of Columbia, Florida, Georgia, Kentucky, Louisiana, Maryland, Mississippi, North Carolina, Oklahoma, South Carolina, Tennessee, Texas, Virginia, and West Virginia

REGION 4 – WEST

Alaska, Arizona, California, Colorado, Hawaii, Idaho, Montana, Nevada, New Mexico, Oregon, Utah, Washington, and Wyoming

LISTS OF COSTUME DESIGN & TECHNICAL THEATRE PROGRAMS

T he programs listed in the following pages include costume design and technical theatre programs. This book also lists the top fashion design, fashion merchandising, drama/theatre, and musical theatre schools since many students interested in costume design and technical theatre are often also interested in all aspects of theatre. There are many facets of the theatre world. One of these other areas might be a good option for you.

Costume design and technical theatre are not for everyone. Although immensely rewarding, the work is sometimes tedious, strenuous, and thankless.

Thus, this book aims to provide you with a more comprehensive set of lists so that you can explore your options. Keep the book handy. Even after you begin college, you may find the additional programs in the back are helpful for connections or summer programs.

Creating lists is often tedious and cumbersome. These lists were gathered to help you with this task.

Descriptions of the college programs, tuition, requirements, and deadlines are accurate as of December 2021. The requirements may have changed somewhat by the time you purchase this book, but this information is a great place to start!

Note: To simplify the text and fit information into the charts and descriptions, abbreviations were used as well as shortened sentences and acronyms.

CONNECTICUT

MAINE

MASSACHUSETTS

NEW HAMPSHIRE

NEW JERSEY

NEW YORK

PENNSYLVANIA

RHODE ISLAND

VERMONT

CHAPTER 13

REGION ONE

NORTHEAST

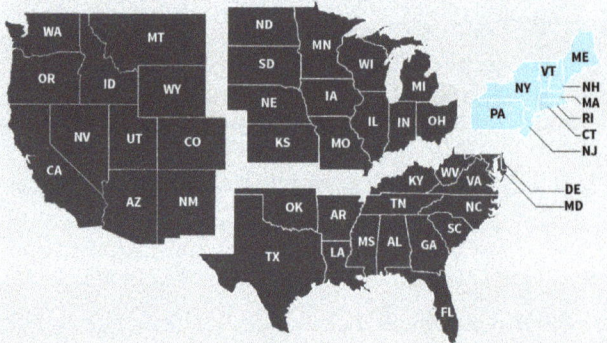

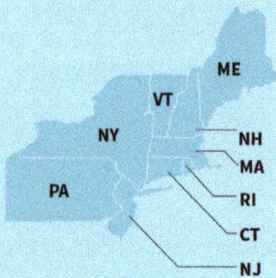

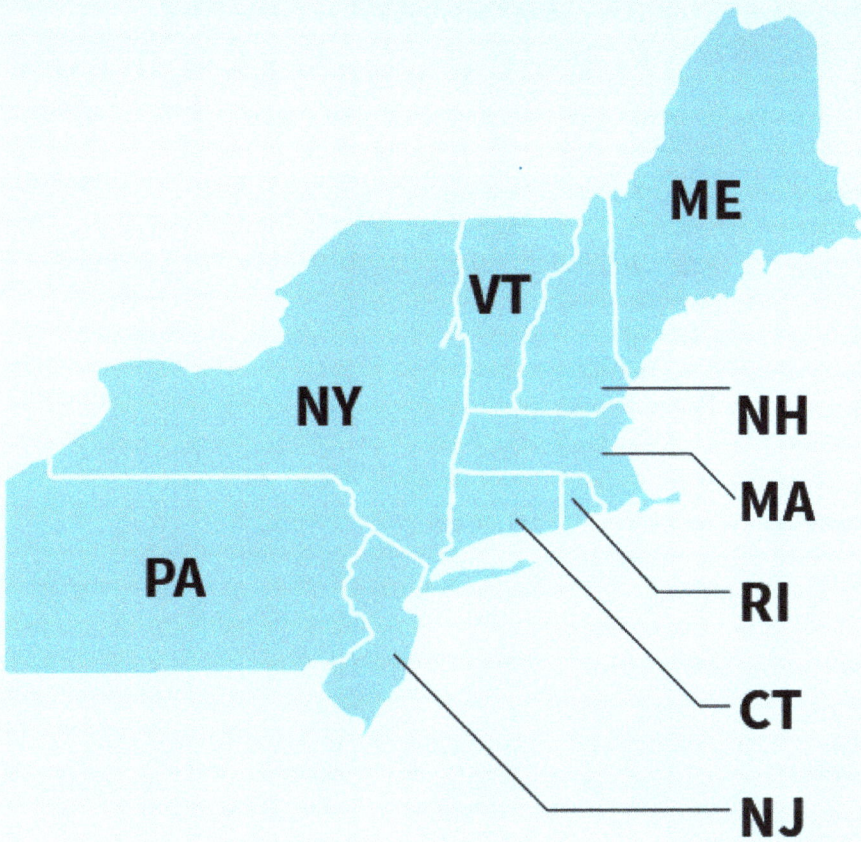

17 Programs | 9 States

1. CT – University of Connecticut (UConn)
2. MA – Boston University (BU)
3. MA – Emerson College
4. NJ – Montclair State University
5. NJ – Rutgers University
6. NY – CUNY NYC College of Technology
7. NY – Ithaca College
8. NY – Marymount Manhattan College
9. NY – Pace University
10. NY – Skidmore College
11. NY – SUNY Binghamton
12. NY – SUNY Purchase
13. NY – Syracuse University
14. NY – University at Buffalo
15. PA – Carnegie Mellon University
16. PA – Pennsylvania State University
17. PA – University of the Arts (UArts)

COSTUME DESIGN & TECHNICAL THEATRE SCHOOLS

School	Avg. GPA, SAT Evidence-Based Reading Writing (ERW), SAT Math (M), and ACT Composite (C) Early Decision (ED): Yes/No	Admission Statistics	Program(s)	Portfolio, Interview, and/or Audition Required (Req.)
University of Connecticut (UConn) University of Connecticut, Storrs, CT 06269	GPA: N/A SAT (ERW): 580-680 SAT (M): 590-710 ACT (C): 27-32 ED: No	Admit Rate: 56% Undergrad Enrollment: 18,917 Total Enrollment: 27,215	BFA Design & Technical Theatre Degrees Awarded in the Program(s) (2020): 12	Portfolio: Req. Interview: Not req. Audition: Not req.
Boston University Boston University, Boston, MA 02215	GPA: 3.76 SAT (ERW): 640-720 SAT (M): 670-780 ACT (C): 30-34 ED: Yes	Admit Rate: 20% Undergrad Enrollment: 16,872 Total Enrollment: 32,718	BFA Costume Design BFA Costume Production BFA Lighting Design BFA Scene Design BFA Sound Design BFA Stage Management BFA Technical Production BFA Theatre Arts BFA Design & Production Degrees Awarded in the Program(s) (2020): 14	Portfolio: Req. Interview: Req. Audition: Not req.

School	Avg. GPA, SAT Evidence-Based Reading Writing (ERW), SAT Math (M), and ACT Composite (C) Early Decision (ED): Yes/No	Admission Statistics	Program(s)	Portfolio, Interview, and/ or Audition Required (Req.)
Emerson College 120 Boylston Street Boston, MA 02116	GPA: 3.5 SAT (ERW): 610-690 SAT (M): 580-690 ACT (C): 27-31 *Emerson College is test optional. ED: Yes	Admit Rate: 41% Undergrad Enrollment: 3,708 Total Enrollment: 5,115	BFA Stage & Production Management BFA Stage & Screen Design/ Technology BFA Theatre Design/ Technology Degrees Awarded in the Program(s) (2020): 43	Portfolio: Req. Interview: Req. Audition: Not req.
Montclair State University 1 Normal Ave., Montclair, NJ 07043	GPA: 3.3 SAT (ERW): 490-590 SAT (M): 490-570 ACT (C): N/A *Montclair State is test optional. ED: No	Admit Rate: 83% Undergrad Enrollment: 16,374 Total Enrollment: 21,005	BFA Theatre, concentration: Design, Technology and Management Degrees Awarded in the Program(s) (2020): 71	Portfolio: Req. Interview: Req. Audition: Not req.

NORTHEAST

COSTUME DESIGN & TECHNICAL THEATRE SCHOOLS

School	Avg. GPA, SAT Evidence-Based Reading Writing (ERW), SAT Math (M), and ACT Composite (C) Early Decision (ED): Yes/No	Admission Statistics	Program(s)	Portfolio, Interview, and/or Audition Required (Req.)
Rutgers University Rutgers University, New Brunswick, NJ 08854	GPA: N/A SAT (ERW): 580-680 SAT (M): 600-730 ACT (C): 25-32 ED: No	Admit Rate: 67% Undergrad Enrollment: 35,844 Total Enrollment: 50,411	BFA Theater, concentrations: *Design* *Production* Areas of study in Design: *Costume Design* *Lighting Design* *Scenic Design* Areas of Study in Production: *Costume Technology* *Stage Management* *Technical Direction* Degrees Awarded in the Program(s) (2020): 34	Portfolio: Req. Interview: Req. Audition: Not req.
CUNY NYC College of Technology 300 Jay St, Brooklyn, NY 11201	GPA: N/A SAT (ERW): N/A SAT (M): N/A ACT (C): N/A ED: No	Admit Rate: 79% Undergrad Enrollment: 15,513 Total Enrollment: 15,513	BTech Entertainment Technology Degrees Awarded in the Program(s) (2020): 38	Portfolio: Not req. Interview: Not req. Audition: Not req.

School	Avg. GPA, SAT Evidence-Based Reading Writing (ERW), SAT Math (M), and ACT Composite (C) Early Decision (ED): Yes/No	Admission Statistics	Program(s)	Portfolio, Interview, and/or Audition Required (Req.)
Ithaca College 953 Danby Road, Ithaca, NY 14850	GPA: N/A SAT (ERW): 590-670 SAT (M): 570-650 ACT (C): 26-31 *Ithaca College is test optional. ED: No	Admit Rate: 76% Undergrad Enrollment: 4,957 Total Enrollment: 5,354	BFA Stage Management BFA Theatre Production & Design BS Theatre Arts Management Degrees Awarded in the Program(s) (2020): 20	Portfolio: Req. Interview: Req. for BS Theatre Arts Management and BFA Stage Management Audition: Not req.
Marymount Manhattan College 221 E 71st St, New York, NY 10021	GPA: N/A SAT (ERW): 500-580 SAT (M): 460-620 ACT (C): 20-28 ED: Yes	Admit Rate: 88% Undergrad Enrollment: 1,722 Total Enrollment: 1,722	BFA Stage and Production Management BFA Theatre Design and Technology, concentrations: Costume Design Lighting Design Scenic Design Sound Design Technical Production Theatrical Media BA Theatre Arts, concentration: Theatre and New Media Degrees Awarded in the Program(s) (2020): 32	Portfolio: Req. Interview: Req. Audition: Not req.

NORTHEAST

COSTUME DESIGN & TECHNICAL THEATRE SCHOOLS

School	Avg. GPA, SAT Evidence-Based Reading Writing (ERW), SAT Math (M), and ACT Composite (C) Early Decision (ED): Yes/No	Admission Statistics	Program(s)	Portfolio, Interview, and/or Audition Required (Req.)
Pace University 1 Pace Plaza, New York, NY 10038	GPA: N/A SAT (ERW): 540-630 SAT (M): 520-610 ACT (C): 22-28 *Pace University is test optional. ED: Yes	Admit Rate: 83% Undergrad Enrollment: 7,994 Total Enrollment: 12,835	BA Stage Management BFA Production and Design for Stage and Screen Degrees Awarded in the Program(s) (2020): 69	Portfolio: Req. Interview: Req. Audition: Not req.
Skidmore College 815 N. Broadway, Saratoga Springs, NY 12866	GPA: N/A SAT (ERW): 610-700 SAT (M): 610-700 ACT (C): 27-31 ED: Yes	Admit Rate: 32% Undergrad Enrollment: 2,582 Total Enrollment: 2,582	BS Theater: Design & Technical Theater Degrees Awarded in the Program(s) (2020): 13	Portfolio: Not req. Interview: Optional Audition: Not req.
SUNY Binghamton 4400 Vestal Pkwy E, Binghamton, NY 13902	GPA: N/A SAT (ERW): 640-710 SAT (M): 650-740 ACT (C): 29-32 ED: No	Admit Rate: 43% Undergrad Enrollment: 14,333 Total Enrollment: 18,148	BA Theatre, concentration: Design/Technical Degrees Awarded in the Program(s) (2020): 9	Portfolio: Optional Interview: Optional Audition: Not req.

School	Avg. GPA, SAT Evidence-Based Reading Writing (ERW), SAT Math (M), and ACT Composite (C) Early Decision (ED): Yes/No	Admission Statistics	Program(s)	Portfolio, Interview, and/or Audition Required (Req.)
SUNY Purchase 735 Anderson Hill Road Purchase, NY 10577, USA	GPA: 3.33 SAT (ERW): 560-660 SAT (M): 540-620 ACT (C): 24-30 ED: No	Admit Rate: 74% Undergrad Enrollment: 3,600 Total Enrollment: 3,685	BFA Theatre Design/ Technology, concentrations: Scenic Design Costume Design Lighting Design Costume Technology Stage Management Technical Direction/ Production Management Degrees Awarded in the Program(s) (2020): 27	Portfolio: Req. Interview: Req. Audition: Not req.
Syracuse University 200 Crouse College, Syracuse, NY 13244	GPA: 3.67 SAT (ERW): 580-670 SAT (M): 600-710 ACT (C): 26-30 ED: Yes	Admit Rate: 69% Undergrad Enrollment: 14,479 Total Enrollment: 21,322	BS Drama Theatre Management Degrees Awarded in the Program(s) (2020): 10	Portfolio: Req. Interview: Req. Audition: Not req.

NORTHEAST

COSTUME DESIGN & TECHNICAL THEATRE SCHOOLS

School	Avg. GPA, SAT Evidence-Based Reading Writing (ERW), SAT Math (M), and ACT Composite (C) Early Decision (ED): Yes/No	Admission Statistics	Program(s)	Portfolio, Interview, and/or Audition Required (Req.)
University at Buffalo 285 Alumni Arena, North Campus Buffalo, New York 14260	GPA: 3.7 SAT (ERW): 560-640 SAT (M): 580-670 ACT (C): 23-29 ED: No	Admit Rate: 67% Undergrad Enrollment: 22,306 Total Enrollment: 32,347	BFA Theatre, concentration: Design and Technology Degrees Awarded in the Program(s) (2020): 19	Portfolio: Req. Interview: Req. Audition: Not req.
Carnegie Mellon University 5000 Forbes Ave, Pittsburgh, PA 15213	GPA: 3.85 SAT (ERW): 700-760 SAT (M): 760-800 ACT (C): 33-35 ED: Yes	Admit Rate: 17% Undergrad Enrollment: 6,622 Total Enrollment: 13,519	BFA Drama Degrees Awarded in the Program(s) (2020): N/A	Portfolio: Req. Interview: Not req. Audition: Not req.
Pennsylvania State University (Penn State) 124 Borland Building, University Park, PA 16802	GPA: N/A SAT (ERW): 530-640 SAT (M): 540-660 ACT (C): 24-29 ED: No	Admit Rate: 78% Undergrad Enrollment: 74,446 Total Enrollment: 89,816	BFA Theatre: Design & Technology BFA Theatre: Stage Management Degrees Awarded in the Program(s) (2020): 16	Portfolio: Req. Interview: Req. Audition: Not req.
University of the Arts (UArts) 320 S. Broad St. Philadelphia, PA 19102	GPA: N/A SAT (ERW): N/A SAT (M): N/A ACT (C): N/A *University of the Arts is test optional. ED: No	Admit Rate: 76% Undergrad Enrollment: 1,380 Total Enrollment: 1,530	BFA Theater Design and Technology Degrees Awarded in the Program(s) (2020): 18	Portfolio: Req. Interview: Req. Audition: Not req.

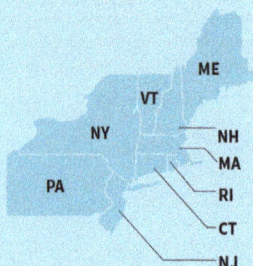

UNIVERSITY OF CONNECTICUT (UCONN)

Address: University of Connecticut, Storrs, CT 06269
Website: https://drama.uconn.edu/programs/design-tech/bfa-design-tech/
Contact: https://drama.uconn.edu/overview/contact/
Request for Information: https://connect.uconn.edu/register/join
Phone: (860)-486-2281
Email: dramaoffice@uconn.edu

COST OF ATTENDANCE:

In-State Tuition & Fees: $18,524 | **Additional Expenses:** $16,214
Total: $34,738

New England Tuition & Fees: $27,542 | **Additional Expenses:** $16,214
Total: $43,756

Out-of-State Tuition & Fees: $41,192 | **Additional Expenses:** $16,214
Total: $57,406

Financial Aid: https://financialaid.uconn.edu/

ADDITIONAL INFORMATION:

Available Degree(s)

- BFA Design & Technical Theatre

Freshman Portfolio Requirement

- Submit via SlideRoom
- 2-15 items, may include: images, videos, audio, PDFs, and models (Sketchfab)
- Must include designs and photos of productions that you've been involved in
- Resume

For more information, visit: https://drama.uconn.edu/apply/

Scholarships Offered

First-year applicants are automatically considered for most merit scholarships offered at the University of Connecticut with the exception of the Nutmeg Scholarship, Day of Pride Scholarship, the President-to-President Scholarship, and UConn Promise Grants. For more information, visit: https://admissions.uconn.edu/cost-aid/financial-aid/

Special Opportunities

Located near New York City, students have access to some of the best regional theatres in the country and receive free tickets to shows. An academic connection to the Metropolitan Opera Hartford Stage and TheatreWorks offer internships and chances to see free performances.

Study abroad opportunities include Bournemouth University College of the Arts and London University Wimbledon College of the Arts in the UK.

Notable Alumni

- Chris Barreca: winner of 2014 Tony Award for Best Lighting Design (*Rocky The Musical*)
- Dan Rousseau: winner of Emmy Award for Outstanding Lighting Direction and Scenic Design (*NBC Nightly News: Decision 2012 – Election Night Coverage from Democracy Plaza*)
- Greg Fuscaldo: Programmer, Broad op and Electrician (*Disney On Ice: Worlds Of Fantasy*)

CONNECTICUT

MAINE

MASSACHUSETTS

NEW HAMPSHIRE

NEW JERSEY

NEW YORK

PENNSYLVANIA

RHODE ISLAND

VERMONT

BOSTON UNIVERSITY

Address: 1 Silber Way, Boston, MA 02215
Website: https://www.bu.edu/cfa/academics/find-a-degreeprogram/school-of-theatre/design-and-production-core/
Contact: https://www.bu.edu/cfa/aboutcfa/contact/
Request for Information: N/A
Phone: (617) 353-3350
Email: Contact via contact link

COST OF ATTENDANCE:

Tuition & Fees: $59,816 | **Additional Expenses:** $19,790
Total: $79,606

Financial Aid: http://www.bu.edu/finaid/

ADDITIONAL INFORMATION:

Available Degree(s)
- BFA Costume Design
- BFA Costume Production
- BFA Lighting Design
- BFA Scenic Design
- BFA Sound Design
- BFA Stage Management
- BFA Technical Production
- BFA Theatre Arts
- BFA Design & Production

Freshman Portfolio Requirement
- Interviews required
- Submit via Acceptd
- 20 files required, including headshot and resume
- Design & Production
- Theatre renderings, working drawings, lighting plots, props, masks, etc.
- Stage Management
- Prompt books, programs, creative writing, director's notes
- Optional supplememt: recommendation letter and 300–500-word response

For more information, visit: https://www.bu.edu/cfa/admissions/school-of-theatre/undergraduate/reviews/portfolio/

For more information, visit: https://www.bu.edu/cfa/admissions/school-of-theatre/undergraduate/reviews/portfolio/

Scholarships Offered
Boston University offers merit-based and need-based aid to all incoming students. A few merit scholarships include the Trustee Scholarship (full tuition and fees), the Presidential Scholarship ($25,000 annually), and the National Merit Scholarship (for National Merit finalists, valued at $25,000 per year). For more information, visit: http://www.bu.edu/finaid/types-of-aid/scholarships-grants/

Special Opportunities
Students in the BFA Stage Management program are required to spend the second semester of the junior year studying abroad through BU Study Abroad.

Notable Alumni
- Stewart F. Lane: Tony Award-winning Broadway producer (*Gentleman's Guide to Love and Murder*)
- Chris Akerlind: winner of Tony Award for Best Lighting Design (*The Light in the Piazza*)
- David Reynoso: Costume Designer (*Sleep No More* NYC)

CONNECTICUT

MAINE

MASSACHUSETTS

NEW HAMPSHIRE

NEW JERSEY

NEW YORK

PENNSYLVANIA

RHODE ISLAND

VERMONT

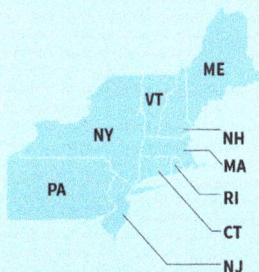

NORTHEAST

CONNECTICUT

MAINE

MASSACHUSETTS

NEW HAMPSHIRE

NEW JERSEY

NEW YORK

PENNSYLVANIA

RHODE ISLAND

VERMONT

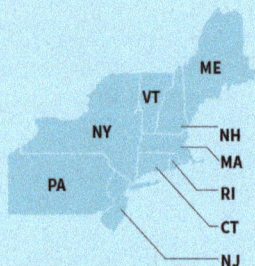

EMERSON COLLEGE

Address: 120 Boylston St., Boston, MA 02116
Website: https://www.emerson.edu/academics/academic-departments/performing-arts/undergraduate-degrees/theatre-designtechnology
Contact: https://www.emerson.edu/contact
Request for Information: https://www.emerson.edu/admissions-aid/undergraduate-admission/request-information
Phone: (617) 824-8500
Email: admission@emerson.edu
Other locations: Los Angeles, CA

COST OF ATTENDANCE:

Tuition & Fees: $51,148 | **Additional Expenses:** $24,788
Total: $75,936

Financial Aid: https://www.emerson.edu/admissions-aid/undergraduate-admission/financial-aid-scholarships

ADDITIONAL INFORMATION:

Available Degree(s)
- BFA Stage & Production Management
- BFA Stage & Screen Design/Technology
- BFA Theatre Design/Technology

Freshman Portfolio Requirement

For all programs,
- Interview required, in person or virtually
- Submit via Acceptd
- Resume & Headshot

BFA Theatre Design/Technology
- 20 creative samples documenting work in theatre
- Sketches, video, audio, paintings, etc.

BFA Stage & Production Management
- Partial production scripts that highlight your work
- Contact sheets, production schedules, etc.

Students interested in the BFA in Stage & Screen Design Technology start in the Theatre Design/Technology degree before choosing Stage & Screen Design/Technology in their second year. For more information, visit: https://www.emerson.edu/academics/academic-departments/performing-arts/undergraduate-degrees/stage-screen-design-technology

Scholarships Offered
The Trustees Scholarship is awarded to students who are accepted into the Honors Program. The award amount is $28,000 per year. For more information, visit: https://www.emerson.edu/admissions-aid/undergraduate-admission/financial-aid-scholarships

Special Opportunities
The College has a producing laboratory, the Emerson Stage. Students have unique access to performance and production spaces including five theatres.

Notable Alumni
- Kevin Bright: Producer (*Friends*) and Founding Director of Emerson Los Angeles
- Eric Falconer: Producer (*How I Met Your Mother, Blue Mountain State, The Sarah Silverman Program*)
- Chris Romano: Producer (*How I Met Your Mother, Blue Mountain State, The Sarah Silverman Program*)

MONTCLAIR STATE UNIVERSITY

Address: 1 Normal Ave., Montclair, NJ 07043
Website: https://www.montclair.edu/theatre-and-dance/academic-programs/undergraduate/bfa-production-and-design/
Contact: https://www.montclair.edu/about-montclair/contact-us/
Request for Information: https://apply.montclair.edu/register/inquire
Phone: (973) 655-4000
Email: msuadm@montclair.edu

COST OF ATTENDANCE:

In-State Tuition & Fees: $13,298 | **Additional Expenses:** $16,388
Total: $26,686

Out-of-State Tuition & Fees: $21,418 | **Additional Expenses:** $16,388
Total: $37,806

Financial Aid: https://www.montclair.edu/admissions/cost-and-financial-aid/affordability/

ADDITIONAL INFORMATION:

Available Degree(s)

- BFA Theatre, concentration: Design, Technology and Management

Freshman Portfolio Requirement

- Interview required
- Essay Response Video (6-10 minutes)
- Resume and headshot
- Include examples of best artwork, production work, and tech/management abilities
- Works should showcase area of interest: management, design, or technical work

For more information, visit: https://www.montclair.edu/theatre-and-dance/admission/admission-bfa-production-and-design/

Scholarships Offered

Montclair State University offers merit-based Presidential Scholarships for in-state, out-of-state, and international students. No separate application is required. For more information, visit: https://www.montclair.edu/admissions/cost-and-financial-aid/affordability/

Special Opportunities

Students can study theatre in London, Greece, and other locations through faculty-led programs and exchange programs. For more information, visit: https://www.montclair.edu/study-abroad/explore-programs/

Notable Alumni

- Kevin Allen: Production Designer (*Money Line* on CNN, CNBC New York and *Larry King Live*)
- Tom Leonardis: Tony-nominated Broadway Producer (*Whoopi: Back to Broadway-The 20th Anniversary*)
- Jill Witte: Emmy Award-winning Lighting Designer for the 2004 Winter Olympics

CONNECTICUT

MAINE

MASSACHUSETTS

NEW HAMPSHIRE

NEW JERSEY

NEW YORK

PENNSYLVANIA

RHODE ISLAND

VERMONT

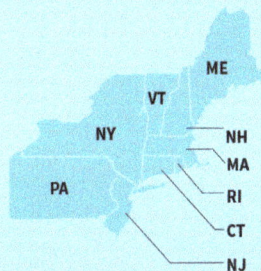

NORTHEAST

CONNECTICUT

MAINE

MASSACHUSETTS

NEW HAMPSHIRE

NEW JERSEY

NEW YORK

PENNSYLVANIA

RHODE ISLAND

VERMONT

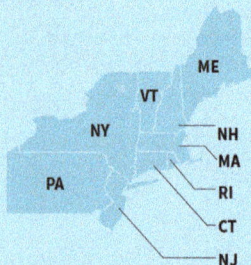

RUTGERS UNIVERSITY

Address: 33 Livingston Avenue, Suite 124, New Brunswick, NJ 08901
Website: https://www.masongross.rutgers.edu/degrees-programs/theater/programs/bfa/
Contact: https://www.masongross.rutgers.edu/admissions/contact
Request for Information: https://www.masongross.rutgers.edu/admissions/contact
Phone: (848) 445-3777
Email: admissions@ugadm.rutgers.edu

COST OF ATTENDANCE:

In-State Tuition & Fees: $15,804 | **Additional Expenses:** $20,631
Total: $36,435

Out-of-State Tuition & Fees: $33,082 | **Additional Expenses:** $20,631
Total: $53,713

Financial Aid: https://financialaid.rutgers.edu/

ADDITIONAL INFORMATION:

Available Degree(s)
- BFA Theater, concentrations:
  - Design, areas of study:
    - Costume Design
    - Lighting Design
    - Scenic Design
  - Production, areas of study:
    - Costume Technology
    - Stage Management
    - Technical Direction

Freshman Portfolio Requirement
- Interview required, on campus or virtually
- Submit via Mason Gross supplemental application
- Stage Management requirements
  - Prompt books, paperwork, examples of theatre work such as productions, craft projects, programs, posters, etc.
- All design areas, Costume Technology, and Technical Direction requirements
  - Designs, drafting, photographs of productions, scenic construction, clothing, paperwork, and non-theatrical artworks

For more information, visit: https://www.masongross.rutgers.edu/degrees-programs/theater/apply/design-production/

Scholarships Offered
Scholarships are awarded on a rolling basis, based on fund availability. The Mason Gross School of the Arts also awards merit scholarships to students. For more information, visit: https://www.masongross.rutgers.edu/admissions/tuition-scholarships

Special Opportunities
All theatre students with a concentration in design spend the fall semester of their third year in London at Shakespeare's Globe. The Costume Technology students also spend the semester studying with designers in London.

Notable Alumni
- Mary Howard: Set and Production Designer
- Keith Sonnier: Light and Video Artist and Performance Artist
- Ray Stark: Film Producer

CUNY NYC COLLEGE OF TECHNOLOGY

Address: 300 Jay St, Brooklyn, NY 11201
Website: https://www.citytech.cuny.edu/entertainment/
entertainment-technology-btech.aspx
Contact: https://www.citytech.cuny.edu/entertainment/
entertainment-technology-btech.aspx
Request for Information: N/A
Phone: (718) 635-2192
Email: entertainmenttechnology@citytech.cuny.edu

COST OF ATTENDANCE:

In-State Tuition & Fees: $6,930 | **Additional Expenses:** N/A
Total: $6,930

Out-of-State Tuition & Fees: $13,860 | **Additional Expenses:** N/A
Total: $13,860

*These figures are an estimate, and come from: https://www.
citytech.cuny.edu/admissions/tuition-general.aspx

Financial Aid: https://www.citytech.cuny.edu/financial-aid/

ADDITIONAL INFORMATION:

Available Degree(s)

- BTech Entertainment Technology

Freshman Portfolio Requirement

There is no portfolio requirement.

Scholarships Offered

Francis Ashworth Scholarship and The Selldorf Architects
Scholarship are established to support students enrolled in School
of Technology & Design majors. Made in New York Scholarship
provides financial support to third-year students enrolled in the
Entertainment Technology program or a related area. City Tech also
offers general scholarships. For more information, visit: https://
www.citytech.cuny.edu/scholarships/scholarships.aspx

Special Opportunities

Students have access to a lighting system laboratory and sound
training facility. A fully equipped performance venue is dedicated
to the Entertainment Technology Department and two laboratories
are dedicated to Emerging Media Technologies: one has the latest
interactive media and software development environments, the
other with a state-of-the-art hardware development facility with
rapid prototyping and 3D printers.

Summer theatre programs are available in London, England and
Japan. For more information, visit: https://travelregistry.cuny.
edu/index.cfm?FuseAction=Programs.SearchResults&Program_
Name=theater&Program_Type_ID=1

CONNECTICUT

MAINE

MASSACHUSETTS

NEW HAMPSHIRE

NEW JERSEY

NEW YORK

PENNSYLVANIA

RHODE ISLAND

VERMONT

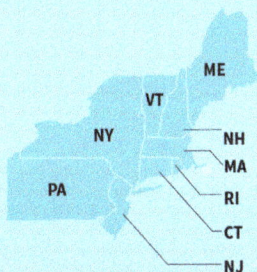

NORTHEAST

CONNECTICUT

MAINE

MASSACHUSETTS

NEW HAMPSHIRE

NEW JERSEY

NEW YORK

PENNSYLVANIA

RHODE ISLAND

VERMONT

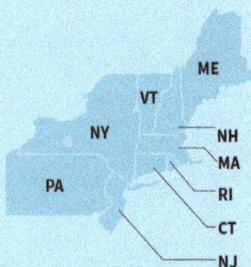

ITHACA COLLEGE

Address: 953 Danby Road, Ithaca, NY 14850
Website: https://www.ithaca.edu/academics/school-humanities-and-sciences/department-theatre-arts
Contact: https://www.ithaca.edu/contact/
Request for Information: https://connect.ithaca.edu/register/inquire
Phone: (607) 274-3011
Email: admission@ithaca.edu

COST OF ATTENDANCE:

Tuition & Fees: $46,610 | **Additional Expenses:** $15,776
Total: $62,386

Financial Aid: https://www.ithaca.edu/tuition-financial-aid

ADDITIONAL INFORMATION:

Available Degree(s)
- BFA Stage Management
- BFA Theatre Production & Design, concentrations:
  o Design
  o Technology
- BS Theatre Arts Management

Freshman Portfolio Requirement

Submit all portfolios via Acceptd.

BFA Stage Management
- Interview required
- 250–300-word passage, up to 2 minutes long
- Resume, headshot, and samples of production work (optional)

BFA Theatre Production & Design Requirements
- Resume, headshot, and personal statement
- Visual Design or Visual Technology Interest
  o 10-20 photos of productions you've designed or mounted
- Sound Design or Sound Technology Interest
  o 1-3 short videos that contain a montage of 3-5 still photos of production set to the music/soundscape

BS Theatre Arts Management
- Interview required
- Resume, headshot, and personal statement

For more information, visit: https://www.ithaca.edu/academics/school-humanities-and-sciences/theatre-arts/interviews-auditions/interview-audition-requirements

Scholarships Offered
The Martin Luther King Scholar Program is for first year students who demonstrate academic talent, community service, and "embody the ideas of Martin Luther King, Jr." For more information, visit: https://www.ithaca.edu/tuition-financial-aid/financial-aid-basics/scholarships/ithaca-scholarships-new-students

Special Opportunities
For more information, visit: https://www.ithaca.edu/academics/school-humanities-and-sciences/theatre-arts/theatre-department-handbook/study-opportunities/london-center-drama-program

Notable Alumni
- Travis Coxson: Broadway Stage Manager (*Dear Evan Hansen*)
- Dominic Barbaro: Production Coordinator at FX Networks
- Jen Caprio: Daytime Emmy award-winning Costume Designer (*Sesame Street*)

MARYMOUNT MANHATTAN COLLEGE

Address: 221 East 71st Street New York, NY 10021
Website: https://www.mmm.edu/academics/theatre-arts/stage-and-production-management-major/index.php
Contact: https://www.mmm.edu/admissions/contact-us/
Request for Information: https://apply.mmm.edu/register/discover
Phone: (212) 517-0430
Email: admissions@mmm.edu

COST OF ATTENDANCE:

Tuition & Fees: $37,410 | **Additional Expenses:** $26,394
Total: $63,804

Financial Aid: https://www.mmm.edu/admissions-and-aid/cost-and-financial-aid/

ADDITIONAL INFORMATION:

Available Degree(s)
- BFA Stage and Production Management
- BFA Theatre Design and Technology, concentrations:
  - Costume Design
  - Lighting Design
  - Scenic Design
  - Sound Design
  - Technical Production
  - Theatrical Media
- BA Theatre Arts, concentration: Theatre and New Media

Freshman Portfolio Requirement
- Interview required for both programs
- Applicants may need the following:
  - Portfolios, prompt books, photographs, drawings, and support materials

For more information, visit: https://www.mmm.edu/admissions-and-aid/fine-and-performing-arts-admission.php

Scholarships Offered
MMC offers the merit-awards for first-year students based equally on SAT/ACT scores and high school GPA. MMC also offers scholarships exclusively for international students who apply with TOEFL or IELTS scores. In addition, MMC offers the Fine and Performing Arts Scholarship, which ranges from $1,000-$10,000 per year. For more information, visit: https://www.mmm.edu/admissions/financial-aid-scholarships.php

Special Opportunities
From the intimate J. William Bordeau Box Theatre to the Great Hall, MMC's Theatre Arts program has a range of performance spaces. Located in the heart of Manhattan, students in the programs experience all that New York City has to offer. Study abroad opportunities at institutes such as the Kingston University London are available via CIEE and CCIS. For more information, visit: https://www.mmm.edu/offices/study-abroad/study-abroad-guide/

Students can combine their BFA or BA degree with an Arts Management Minor.

Notable Alumni
- Aaron Glick: Theatrical Producer (*The Boys in the Band*)

CONNECTICUT

MAINE

MASSACHUSETTS

NEW HAMPSHIRE

NEW JERSEY

NEW YORK

PENNSYLVANIA

RHODE ISLAND

VERMONT

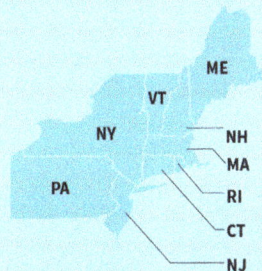

NORTHEAST

CONNECTICUT

MAINE

MASSACHUSETTS

NEW HAMPSHIRE

NEW JERSEY

NEW YORK

PENNSYLVANIA

RHODE ISLAND

VERMONT

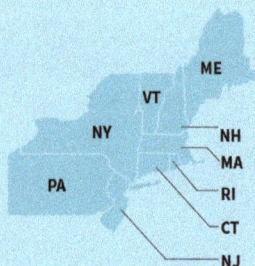

PACE UNIVERSITY

Address: 1 Pace Plaza, New York, NY 10038
Website: https://www.pace.edu/program/production-and-design-stage-and-screen-bfa
Contact: https://www.pace.edu/contact-us
Request for Information: https://admission.pace.edu/register/request-information
Phone: (866) 722-3338
Email: undergradadmission@pace.edu

COST OF ATTENDANCE:

Tuition & Fees: $53,940 | **Additional Expenses:** $23,174
Total: $77,114

Financial Aid: https://www.pace.edu/financial-aid/

ADDITIONAL INFORMATION:

Available Degree(s)

- BA in Stage Management
- BFA in Production and Design for Stage and Screen

Freshman Portfolio Requirement

BA in Stage Management
- Submit via Acceptd
- Interview required, in-person or virtually
- Resume
- Portfolio that includes relevant material of you as a stage manager
  o Prompt book, contact sheets, etc.
- 1 wild card video (optional)

BFA Production and Design for Stage and Screen
- Submit via Acceptd
- Interview required, in-person or virtually
- Resume
- Portfolio that includes relevant material of you as a designer or stage technician
- 1 wild card video (optional)

For more information, visit: https://performingarts.pace.edu/auditioninterview-requirements

Scholarships Offered
Pace offers two institutional grants: The Pace Grant and the Trustee Tuition Grant ($500). They also offer several merit scholarships that are renewable. These scholarships include the Honors College Scholarship, Honors Opportunity Scholarship, President's Scholarship, Trustee Recognition Award, and Pace Incentive Award. For more information, visit: https://www.pace.edu/financial-aid/types-financial-aid/scholarships-grants

Special Opportunities
The program is based in New York City, one of the world's great epicenters for performing arts. Students can combine their BFA or BA degree with a BBA or minor in Arts and Entertainment Management.

Notable Alumni
- David Shocket: Lighting Designer (*What the Constitution Means to Me*)

SKIDMORE COLLEGE

Address: 815 N. Broadway, Saratoga Springs, NY 12866
Website: https://theater.skidmore.edu/
Contact: https://www.skidmore.edu/about/contacts.php
Request for Information: https://www.skidmore.edu/admissions/info/index.php
Phone: (518) 580-5430
Email: admissions@skidmore.edu

COST OF ATTENDANCE:

Tuition & Fees: $60,152 | **Additional Expenses:** $16,068
Total: $76,220

Financial Aid: https://www.skidmore.edu/financialaid/

ADDITIONAL INFORMATION:

Available Degree(s)

- BS Theater: Design & Technical Theater

Freshman Portfolio Requirement

There is no portfolio requirement.

Scholarships Offered

Funded by internal grants and scholarships, federal, state, and independent programs, most of the financial assistance at Skidmore is awarded based on need and usually includes a grant, campus job, and loan. For more information, visit: https://www.skidmore.edu/financialaid/

Special Opportunities

Skidmore's Summer Theater Workshop with SITI Company is open to high school graduates, matriculated college students, and adults. Skidmore also offers summer classes including Introduction to Shakespeare, Introduction to Media Studies, and Screenwriting. For more information, visit: https://www.skidmore.edu/summersession/

Theater students may study abroad in Italy, Ireland, Russia, and England. Each year, 36 freshmen spend their first semester of college in London, where they can take classes including Theatre in London: An Introduction. For more information, visit: https://www.skidmore.edu/ocse/london_fye/courses.php

Notable Alumni

- David Miner: Producer, Winner of three Emmy Awards for Outstanding Comedy Series (*30 Rock*)

CONNECTICUT

MAINE

MASSACHUSETTS

NEW HAMPSHIRE

NEW JERSEY

NEW YORK

PENNSYLVANIA

RHODE ISLAND

VERMONT

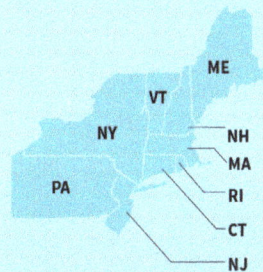

NORTHEAST

CONNECTICUT

MAINE

MASSACHUSETTS

NEW HAMPSHIRE

NEW JERSEY

NEW YORK

PENNSYLVANIA

RHODE ISLAND

VERMONT

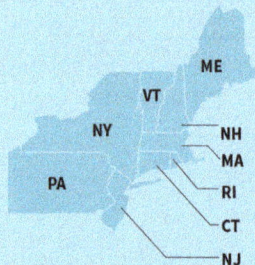

SUNY BINGHAMTON

Address: 4400 Vestal Pkwy E, Binghamton, NY 13902
Website: https://www.binghamton.edu/theatre/undergraduate/index.html
Contact: https://www.binghamton.edu/theatre/contact/
Request for Information: https://www.binghamton.edu/admissions/contact/information.html
Phone: (607) 777-2567
Email: theatre@binghamton.edu

COST OF ATTENDANCE:

In-State Tuition & Fees: $10,319 | **Additional Expenses:** $19,064
Total: $29,383

Out-of-State Tuition & Fees: $28,159 | **Additional Expenses:** $19,264
Total: $47,423

Financial Aid: https://www.binghamton.edu/financial-aid/

ADDITIONAL INFORMATION:

Available Degree(s)

- BA Theatre, concentration: Design/Technical

Freshman Portfolio Requirement

- Portfolios are optional
- Special talent form required
- Resume, 2 letters of recommendation, and personal statement
- Photographs/sketches of your design or construction projects
- Stage work experience and/or stage design drawings

For more information, visit: https://www.binghamton.edu/admissions/apply/freshman/special-talent-theatre-and-dance.html

Scholarships Offered

All students are considered for the President's, Provost's, and Dean's Scholarships. There are also departmental scholarships: The John and Vi Bielenberg Theatre Scholarship is awarded to a sophomore or junior majoring in Theatre with exceptional promise in technical theatre. The Solomon Israel Theatre Arts Scholarship is awarded to a Theatre major from the metropolitan New York area with proven financial need. For more information, visit: https://www.binghamton.edu/theatre/undergraduate/scholarships.html

Special Opportunities

There is an accelerated degree program which allows students to complete a BA and a MPA in Public Administration in just 5 years. For more information, visit: https://www.binghamton.edu/public-administration/academics/accelerated-programs.html

Notable Alumni

- Madeleine Smithberg: Producer (*The Daily Show, Steve Harvey's Big Time Challenge*)
- Neil Berg: Producer (*Neil Berg's 100 Years of Broadway*)
- Todd Lituchy: Producer (*The Mysteries of Laura*)

SUNY PURCHASE

Address: 735 Anderson Hill Road, Purchase, NY 10577
Website: https://www.purchase.edu/academics/theatre-design-technology/
Contact: https://www.purchase.edu/about/contact-us/
Request for Information: https://admission.purchase.edu/register/inquiryform
Phone: (914) 251-6300
Email: purchaseadmissions@purchase.edu

COST OF ATTENDANCE:

In-State Tuition & Fees: $8,556 | **Additional Expenses:** $19,068
Total: $27,694

Out-of-State Tuition & Fees: $18,8466 | **Additional Expenses:** $19,068
Total: $37,604

Financial Aid: https://www.purchase.edu/offices/student-financial-services/financial-aid/

ADDITIONAL INFORMATION:

Available Degree(s)
- BFA Theatre Design/Technology, concentrations:
  - Scenic Design
  - Costume Design
  - Lighting Design
  - Costume Technology
  - Stage Management
  - Technical Direction/Production Management

Freshman Portfolio Requirement
- Submit via Purchase Admissions Portal
- Interview required, in-person
- Headshot and theatrical resume
- 1 letter of recommendation
- Portfolio with examples of design and/or technical work

For more information, visit: https://www.purchase.edu/admissions/audition-and-portfolio-guidelines/theatre-design-technology/

Scholarships Offered
BFA candidates are awarded scholarships based on talent demonstrated during the application process. Scholarships may range from $200 to full tuition. Purchase College also connects students with several outside scholarship opportunities, such as the Elks National Foundation Most Valuable Student Scholarship or the Horatio Alger Scholarships. For more information, visit: https://www.purchase.edu/offices/student-financial-services/financial-aid/scholarships/

Special Opportunities
Located close to New York City, students have easy access to some of the best theatrical venues and production facilities in the country. Purchase College's Performing Arts Center provides students with technical and design resources.

Notable Alumni
- Suzanne McCabe: Costume Designer (*Nurse Jackie; Something's Gotta Give; When it's Over*)
- Thom Widmann: Stage Manager (*Wicked; Light in the Piazza; Contact; Sound of Music*)
- James Youmans: Scenic Designer (*West Side Story; Gypsy; Come Fly Away*)

CONNECTICUT

MAINE

MASSACHUSETTS

NEW HAMPSHIRE

NEW JERSEY

NEW YORK

PENNSYLVANIA

RHODE ISLAND

VERMONT

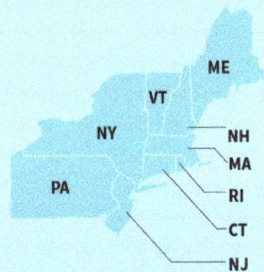

NORTHEAST

SYRACUSE UNIVERSITY

Address: 200 Crouse College, Syracuse, NY 13244
Website: https://vpa.syr.edu/academics/drama/
Contact: https://vpa.syr.edu/academics/drama/contact/
Request for Information: https://vpa.syr.edu/admissions/request-information/
Phone: (315) 443-2769
Email: admissu@syr.edu

COST OF ATTENDANCE:

Tuition & Fees: $54,270 | **Additional Expenses:** $18,012
Total: $72,282

Financial Aid: https://www.syracuse.edu/admissions/cost-and-aid/

ADDITIONAL INFORMATION:

Available Degree(s)
- BS Drama, concentration: Theater Management
- BFA Stage Management
- BFA Theater Design and Technology

Freshman Portfolio Requirement
All programs listed here require a theatrical resume, an interview, and submission via SlideRoom.

BS in Drama: Theater Management Track requirements:
- Statement of Interest

BFA Stage Management requirements:
- Brief statement
- 3 letters of reference from directors, theatre teachers, or technical directors
- Portfolio including samples of stage management production materials

BFA Theater Design and Technology requirements:
- 10-15 examples of work, including but not limited to: drawings, paintings, light plots, CAD drawings, photography, 3D work, production paperwork, thought process sheets, video clips, etc.

For more information, visit: https://vpa.syr.edu/admissions/undergraduate/drama/

Scholarships Offered
Artistic scholarships are awarded to students based on talent and require a maintained cumulative GPA of 2.75+. The Distinguished Art Portfolio Award offers $10,000 awards annually. There is also the Tepper Semester Grant. For more information, visit: https://financialaid.syr.edu/scholarships/

Special Opportunities
The Tepper Semester allows students in theatre to work with professional artists in New York City. Students interested in a longer-term introduction to Los Angeles may participate in Summer in LA, a six-week, two-course experience that includes a professional internship and a series of workshops and master classes.

Notable Alumni
- Tony Walton: Emmy, Academy, and Tony Award-winning Designer
- Joan Schirle: Founding Artistic Director of the Dell'Arte Company

CONNECTICUT

MAINE

MASSACHUSETTS

NEW HAMPSHIRE

NEW JERSEY

NEW YORK

PENNSYLVANIA

RHODE ISLAND

VERMONT

ME
VT
NY
NH
MA
PA
RI
CT
NJ

UNIVERSITY AT BUFFALO

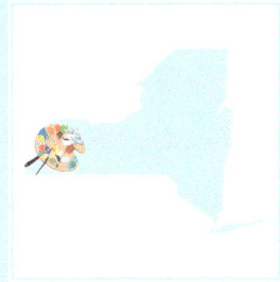

Address: 285 Alumni Arena, North Campus, Buffalo, New York 14260
Website: https://arts-sciences.buffalo.edu/theatre-dance/
undergraduate/bfa-theatre-design-technology.html
Contact: https://arts-sciences.buffalo.edu/theatre-dance/about/
contact-us.html
Request for Information: https://admissions.buffalo.edu/request-
info.php
Phone: (716) 645-6897
Email: td-theatredance@buffalo.edu

COST OF ATTENDANCE:

In-State Tuition & Fees: $10,724 | **Additional Expenses:** $18,142
Total: $28,866

Out-of-State Tuition & Fees: $28,194 | **Additional Expenses:** $18,142
Total: $46,336

Financial Aid: https://financialaid.buffalo.edu/

ADDITIONAL INFORMATION:

Available Degree(s)

- BFA Theatre, concentration: Design and Technology

Freshman Portfolio Requirement

- Interview required
- Portfolio review required

For more information, visit: https://arts-sciences.buffalo.edu/
theatre-dance/undergraduate/admissions.html

Scholarships Offered

University at Buffalo offers various merit-based and need-based
scholarships and grants including the Presidential Scholarship,
Provost Scholarship, and Daniel Acker Scholarship. For more
information, visit: https://admissions.buffalo.edu/costs/
scholarships.php.

Special Opportunities

UB's Department of Theatre and Dance offers a 16-day Play and
Places summer program in Dublin, Ireland and a Culture and
Performance Appreciation winter program in London. Theatre
students may also study abroad at Lorenzo de' Medici in Florence,
Italy or participate in exchange programs at Monash University in
Melbourne, Australia and University of Kent in Canterbury, England.
For more information, visit: https://buffalo-sa.terradotta.com/index.
cfm?FuseAction=Programs.AdvancedSearch

Notable Alumni

- Thomas Curley: winner of Academy Award for Best Sound
  and BAFTA Award for Best Sound (*Whiplash*)

CONNECTICUT

MAINE

MASSACHUSETTS

NEW HAMPSHIRE

NEW JERSEY

NEW YORK

PENNSYLVANIA

RHODE ISLAND

VERMONT

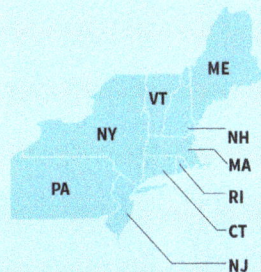

NORTHEAST

CONNECTICUT

MAINE

MASSACHUSETTS

NEW HAMPSHIRE

NEW JERSEY

NEW YORK

PENNSYLVANIA

RHODE ISLAND

VERMONT

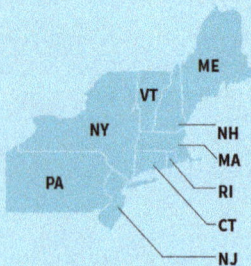

CARNEGIE MELLON UNIVERSITY

Address: 5000 Forbes Avenue, Pittsburgh, PA 15213
Website: https://www.drama.cmu.edu/programs/undergraduate/design-costume/
Contact: https://admission.enrollment.cmu.edu/pages/contact-us
Request for Information: https://admission.cmu.edu/register/connect
Phone: (412) 268-2082
Email: admission@andrew.cmu.edu

Cost of Attendance:

Tuition & Fees: $57,560 | **Additional Expenses:** $19,914
Total: $77,474

Financial Aid: https://www.cmu.edu/admission/aid-affordability

Additional Information:

Available Degree(s)

- BFA Drama, options in:
  - Costume Design
  - Lighting Design
  - Scenic Design
  - Sound Design
  - Production Technology
  - Stage and Production Management
  - Technical Direction

Freshman Portfolio Requirement

- Submit via Acceptd
- Demonstrate basic proficiency in design, project planning, and execution
- 15 examples of work, including but not limited to: sculptures, mechanical drawings, sound cues, etc.

For more information, visit: https://app.getacceptd.com/cmudrama

Scholarships Offered

CMU offers a need-based grant and endowed scholarships. For more information, visit: https://www.cmu.edu/sfs/financial-aid/types/scholarships-and-grants/index.html

Special Opportunities

CMU's School of Drama offers exchange programs at the National School of Drama in India and the Royal Conservatoire of Scotland.

Notable Alumni

- Peter Hylenski: 8-time Tony Award for Best Sound Design nominee
- Peggy Eisenhauer: winner of Tony Award for Best Lighting Design, Broadway Lighting Designer (*Bring in 'Da Noise, Bring in 'Da Funk, Assassins, Lucky Guy*)
- Eduardo Castro: winner of Costumer's Guild Lifetime Achievement Award (*Once Upon a Time, Ugly Betty, Their Eyes Were Watching God*)

PENNSYLVANIA STATE UNIVERSITY (PENN STATE)

Address: 124 Borland Building, University Park, PA 16802
Website: https://theatre.psu.edu/
Contact: https://admissions.psu.edu/contact/
Request for Information: https://arts.psu.edu/request-information/
Phone: (814) 865-2591
Email: admissions@psu.edu

COST OF ATTENDANCE:

In-State Tuition & Fees: $18,898 | **Additional Expenses:** $14,158
Total: $33,056

Out-of-State Tuition & Fees: $36,476 | **Additional Expenses:** $14,158
Total: $50,634

Financial Aid: https://studentaid.psu.edu/

ADDITIONAL INFORMATION:

Available Degree(s)

- BFA Theatre, concentrations:
  - Design & Technology
  - Stage Management

Freshman Portfolio Requirement

- Interview required
- Submit via Acceptd
- Resume and 2 artistic references
- Stage Management Option: portfolio of production notes, pictures, process documentation that show your stage managing and production experience
- Design + Technology Option: portfolio that demonstrates artistic and technical abilities and supplemental essay

For more information, visit: https://arts.psu.edu/how-to-apply/#specific

Scholarships Offered

Penn State offers various university scholarships including the Discover Penn State Award ($6,000-6,500 annually) and the Provost's Award ($5,000 annually) as well as campus and and college scholarships. For more information, visit: https://studentaid.psu.edu/types-of-aid/scholarships

Special Opportunities

Penn State houses state-of-the-art theatre facilities, among which the Lightning Lab is one of the most advanced and well-equipped labs of its kind in the country. Additionally, students also have access to the Theatre Arts Production Studio, Pavilion Theatre, Penn State Downtown Theatre, and the Playhouse Theatre.

Notable Alumni

- Rick Lyon: Puppeteer and Puppet Designer (*Sesame Street and Avenue Q*)
- Carrie Fishbein: Broadway Costume Designer
- Oliver Smith: Broadway Set Designer

CONNECTICUT

MAINE

MASSACHUSETTS

NEW HAMPSHIRE

NEW JERSEY

NEW YORK

PENNSYLVANIA

RHODE ISLAND

VERMONT

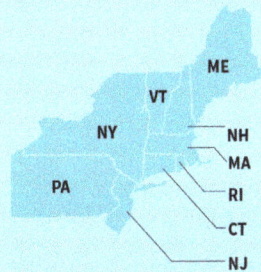

NORTHEAST

CONNECTICUT

MAINE

MASSACHUSETTS

NEW HAMPSHIRE

NEW JERSEY

NEW YORK

PENNSYLVANIA

RHODE ISLAND

VERMONT

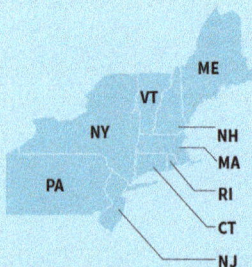

UNIVERSITY OF THE ARTS (UARTS)

Address: 320 S. Broad Street, Philadelphia, PA 19102
Website: https://www.uarts.edu/academics/theater-design-and-technology
Contact: https://www.uarts.edu/about/contact-us
Request for Information: https://www.uarts.edu/admissions/request-more-information
Phone: (215) 717-6049
Email: admissions@uarts.edu

COST OF ATTENDANCE:

Tuition & Fees: $48,350 | **Additional Expenses:** $21,644
Total: $69,994
Financial Aid: https://www.uarts.edu/tuition-and-financial-aid

ADDITIONAL INFORMATION:

Available Degree(s)

- BFA Theater Design and Technology

Freshman Portfolio Requirement

- Interview required
- Submit via Acceptd
- In-person or virtual audition required
- 15-20 pieces of original work
  - Past theatre work, sketches, drafting, model photos, costume process, lighting plots, etc.

For more information, visit: https://www.uarts.edu/admissions/undergraduate-theater-audition-requirements

Scholarships Offered

All applicants including international students are automatically considered for numerous scholarships. Scholarships dedicated to the Ira Brind School of Theater Arts include the Ira Brind Scholarship and the Jac and Miriam Striezheff Lewis Scholarship. For more information, visit: https://www.uarts.edu/about/scholarships

Special Opportunities

Students have access to five public performance venues, the Center for Immersive Media, and other facilities.

High school students may take college-level summer courses including Film & Story Analysis, Directing, Playwriting and Production, Live Sound, Visual Storytelling. UArts also hosts Saturday School for high school students. The curriculum includes Figure Drawing, Graphic Design, Illustration: Setting the Scene, and online or in-person Portfolio Preparation. For more information, visit: https://www.uarts.edu/academics/pre-college-programs

UArts offers Theater students exchange and affiliated programs in London, Moscow, and Dublin. For more information, visit: https://www.uarts.edu/sites/default/files/2017-08/study_abroad_program_options.pdf

ME
VT
NY
NH
MA
PA
RI
CT
NJ

ILLINOIS

INDIANA

IOWA

KANSAS

MICHIGAN

MINNESOTA

MISSOURI

NEBRASKA

NORTH DAKOTA

OHIO

SOUTH DAKOTA

WISCONSIN

CHAPTER 14

REGION TWO

MIDWEST

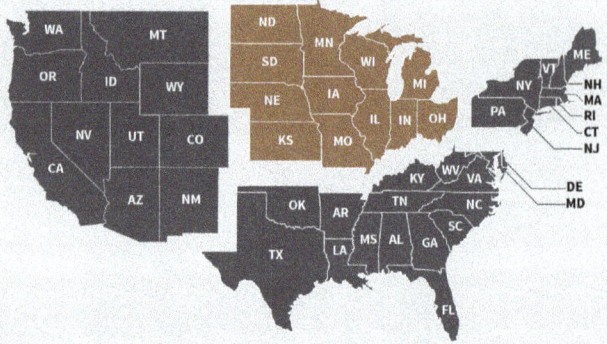

16 *Programs* | 12 *States*

1. *IL – Columbia College Chicago*	**9.** *KS – Wichita State University*
2. *IL – DePaul University*	**10.** *MI – University of Michigan*
3. *IL – Northwestern University*	**11.** *MO – Missouri State University*
4. *IL – University of Illinois, Urbana-Champaign (UIUC)*	**12.** *MO – University of Missouri*
	13. *OH – Baldwin Wallace University*
5. *IN – Ball State University*	**14.** *OH – Kent State University*
6. *IN – Indiana University at Bloomington*	**15.** *OH – University of Cincinnati*
7. *IN – Purdue University*	**16.** *WI – University of Wisconsin*
8. *IN – University of Evansville*	

COSTUME DESIGN & TECHNICAL THEATRE SCHOOLS

School	Avg. GPA, SAT Evidence-Based Reading Writing (ERW), SAT Math (M), and ACT Composite (C) Early Decision (ED): Yes/No	Admission Statistics	Program(s)	Portfolio, Interview, and/ or Audition Required (Req.)
Columbia College Chicago 600 S Michigan Ave, Chicago, IL 60605	GPA: N/A SAT (ERW): N/A SAT (M): N/A ACT (C): N/A *Columbia College Chicago is test optional. ED: No	Admit Rate: 90% Undergrad Enrollment: 6,542 Total Enrollment: 6,769	BA Theatre Design and Technology BA Theatre, concentration: Stage Management Degrees Awarded in the Program(s) (2020): 68	Portfolio: Req. Interview: Not req. Audition: Not req.
DePaul University 2350 N. Racine Ave., Chicago, IL 60614	GPA: 3.8 SAT (ERW): 530-640 SAT (M): 530-640 ACT (C): N/A ED: No	Admit Rate: 70% Undergrad Enrollment: 14,145 Total Enrollment: 21,922	BFA Costume Design BFA Costume Technology BFA Lighting Design BFA Projection Design BFA Scene Design BFA Sound Design BFA Stage Management BFA Theatre Technology BFA Wig and Makeup Design & Technology Degrees Awarded in the Program(s) (2020): 23	Portfolio: Req. Interview: Req. Audition: Not req.

School	Avg. GPA, SAT Evidence-Based Reading Writing (ERW), SAT Math (M), and ACT Composite (C) Early Decision (ED): Yes/No	Admission Statistics	Program(s)	Portfolio, Interview, and/or Audition Required (Req.)
Northwestern University 633 Clark St, Evanston, IL 60208	GPA: N/A SAT (ERW): 700-760 SAT (M): 730-790 ACT (C): 33-35 ED: Yes	Admit Rate: 9% Undergrad Enrollment: 8,559 Total Enrollment: 22,603	BA Theatre, area of study: Design & Stage Management Degrees Awarded in the Program(s) (2020): N/A	Portfolio: Not req. Interview: Not req. Audition: Not req.
University of Illinois Urbana-Champaign (UIUC) 901 West Illinois Street, Urbana, IL 61801	GPA: N/A SAT (ERW): 590-690 SAT (M): 610-770 ACT (C): 27-33 ED: No	Admit Rate: 63% Undergrad Enrollment: 33,683 Total Enrollment: 52,679	BFA Theatre, concentrations: Arts & Entertainment Technology Costume Design & Technology Lighting Design & Technology Scenic Design Scenic Technology Sound Design & Technology Stage Management Degrees Awarded in the Program(s) (2020): 32	Portfolio: Req. Interview: Req. Audition: Not req.

MIDWEST

COSTUME DESIGN & TECHNICAL THEATRE SCHOOLS

School	Avg. GPA, SAT Evidence-Based Reading Writing (ERW), SAT Math (M), and ACT Composite (C) Early Decision (ED): Yes/No	Admission Statistics	Program(s)	Portfolio, Interview, and/ or Audition Required (Req.)
Ball State University 2000 W University Ave, Muncie, IN 47306	GPA: 3.52 SAT (ERW): N/A SAT (M): N/A ACT (C): N/A *Ball State is test optional. ED: No	Admit Rate: 87% Undergrad Enrollment: 15,780 Total Enrollment: 21,597	BA/BS in Theatre: Design and Technology BFA in Theatre: Design and Technology BA or BS in Theatre: Directing and Stage Management BA or BS in Theatre, Theatre Creation option Degrees Awarded in the Program(s) (2020): 70	Portfolio: Req. Interview: Req. for BFA, encouraged for other programs Audition: Not req.
Indiana University at Bloomington 107 S. Indiana Avenue, Bloomington, IN 47405	GPA: 3.75 SAT (ERW): 560-670 SAT (M): 560-680 ACT (C): 24-31 *Indiana University at Bloomington is test optional. ED: No	Admit Rate: 80% Undergrad Enrollment: 32,986 Total Enrollment: 43,064	BA Theatre: Design/ Technology, Emphasis: Stage Management Degrees Awarded in the Program(s) (2020): N/A	Portfolio: Not req. Interview: Not req. Audition: Not req.

School	Avg. GPA, SAT Evidence-Based Reading Writing (ERW), SAT Math (M), and ACT Composite (C) Early Decision (ED): Yes/No	Admission Statistics	Program(s)	Portfolio, Interview, and/or Audition Required (Req.)
Purdue University Purdue University, West Lafayette, IN 47907	GPA: 3.67 SAT (ERW): 580-680 SAT (M): 590-740 ACT (C): 25-33 ED: No	Admit Rate: 67% Undergrad Enrollment: 35,706 Total Enrollment: 46,655	BA Sound for the Performing Arts Degrees Awarded in the Program(s) (2020): 4	Portfolio: Not req. Interview: Not req. Audition: Not req.
University of Evansville 1800 Lincoln Ave, Evansville, IN 47722	GPA: N/A SAT (ERW): N/A SAT (M): N/A ACT (C): N/A *University of Evansville is test optional. ED: No	Admit Rate: 64% Undergrad Enrollment: 2,041 Total Enrollment: 2,323	BFA in Theatre Design and Technology BS in Theatre Design and Technology BS in Stage Management BS in Theatre Management Degrees Awarded in the Program(s) (2020): 5	Portfolio: Req. Interview: Req. Audition: Not req.

MIDWEST

COSTUME DESIGN & TECHNICAL THEATRE SCHOOLS

School	Avg. GPA, SAT Evidence-Based Reading Writing (ERW), SAT Math (M), and ACT Composite (C) Early Decision (ED): Yes/No	Admission Statistics	Program(s)	Portfolio, Interview, and/or Audition Required (Req.)
Wichita State University 1845 Fairmount St, Wichita, KS 67260	GPA: 3.51 SAT (ERW): 510-620 SAT (M): 510-630 ACT (C): 20-27 ED: No	Admit Rate: 80% Undergrad Enrollment: 11,946 Total Enrollment: 14,999	BFA Theatre Design & Technology, specializations: Lighting Design Sound Design Costume Design Set Design Scenic Technology Degrees Awarded in the Program(s) (2020): N/A	Portfolio: Req. Interview: Not req. but encouraged Audition: Not req.
University of Michigan 500 S. State St., Ann Arbor, MI 48109	GPA: 3.87 SAT (ERW): 660-740 SAT (M): 680-780 ACT (C): 31-34 ED: No	Admit Rate: 26% Undergrad Enrollment: 31,329 Total Enrollment: 47,907	BFA Design & Production BFA in Performing Arts Technology Degrees Awarded in the Program(s) (2020): 9	Portfolio: Req. Interview: Req. Audition: Not req.
Missouri State University 901 S National Ave, Springfield, MO 65897	GPA: 3.73 SAT (ERW): 510-610 SAT (M): 510-610 ACT (C): 21-27 ED: No	Admit Rate: 87% Undergrad Enrollment: 19,621 Total Enrollment: 23,505	BFA Design, Technology, and Stage Management Degrees Awarded in the Program(s) (2020): 31	Portfolio: Req. Interview: Not req. for admission but req. for scholarship consideration Audition: Not req.

School	Avg. GPA, SAT Evidence-Based Reading Writing (ERW), SAT Math (M), and ACT Composite (C) Early Decision (ED): Yes/No	Admission Statistics	Program(s)	Portfolio, Interview, and/or Audition Required (Req.)
University of Missouri University of Missouri, Columbia, MO 65211	GPA: N/A SAT (ERW): 560-660 SAT (M): 550-660 ACT (C): 23-29 ED: No	Admit Rate: 82% Undergrad Enrollment: 23,383 Total Enrollment: 31,089	BA in Theatre, concentration: Design/Technical Degrees Awarded in the Program(s) (2020): 11	Portfolio: Not req. Interview: Not req. Audition: Not req.
Baldwin Wallace University 275 Eastland Rd, Berea, OH 44017	GPA: 3.64 SAT (ERW): 520-640 SAT (M): 520-620 ACT (C): 21-27 ED: No	Admit Rate: 70% Undergrad Enrollment: 2,860 Total Enrollment: 3,399	BA Theatre, concentrations: Design & Technical Stage Management Degrees Awarded in the Program(s) (2020): 5	Portfolio: Not req. Interview: Optional, strongly encouraged Audition: Not req.
Kent State University 1325 Theatre Drive, Kent, OH 44242	GPA: 3.61 SAT (ERW): 510-610 SAT (M): 510-600 ACT (C): 20-26 ED: No	Admit Rate: 84% Undergrad Enrollment: 21,621 Total Enrollment: 26,822	BFA Design Technology & Production Degrees Awarded in the Program(s) (2020): 3	Portfolio: Not req. Interview: Not req. Audition: Not req.

MIDWEST

COSTUME DESIGN & TECHNICAL THEATRE SCHOOLS

School	Avg. GPA, SAT Evidence-Based Reading Writing (ERW), SAT Math (M), and ACT Composite (C) Early Decision (ED): Yes/No	Admission Statistics	Program(s)	Portfolio, Interview, and/ or Audition Required (Req.)
University of Cincinnati 2600 Clifton Ave, Cincinnati, OH 45221	GPA: 3.7 SAT (ERW): 560-650 SAT (M): 560-680 ACT (C): 23-29 ED: No	Admit Rate: 76% Undergrad Enrollment: 29,933 Total Enrollment: 40,826	BFA in Theatre Design and Production, concentrations: Costume Design and Technology Lighting Design and Technology Sound Design Stage Design, Props and Scenic Art Stage Management Technical Production Degrees Awarded in the Program(s) (2020): 27	Portfolio: Req. Interview: Req. Audition: Not req.
University of Wisconsin 821 University Ave., 6173 Vilas Hall, Madison, WI 53706	GPA: 3.87 SAT (ERW): 610-690 SAT (M): 650-770 ACT (C): 27-32 ED: No	Admit Rate: 57% Undergrad Enrollment: 32,688 Total Enrollment: 44,640	BS Theatre and Drama (informal emphases: design, stage management, theatre technology) Degrees Awarded in the Program(s) (2020): 8	Portfolio: Not req. Interview: Not req. Audition: Not req.

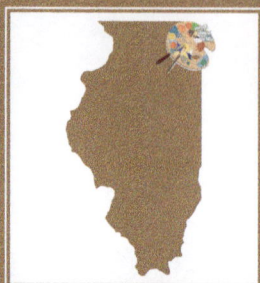

ILLINOIS

INDIANA

IOWA

KANSAS

MICHIGAN

MINNESOTA

MISSOURI

NEBRASKA

NORTH DAKOTA

OHIO

SOUTH DAKOTA

WISCONSIN

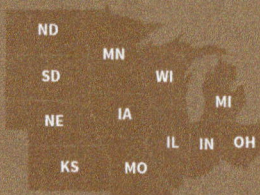

COLUMBIA COLLEGE CHICAGO

Address: 600 S. Michigan Avenue, Chicago, IL 60605
Website: https://www.colum.edu/academics/fine-and-performing-arts/theatre/majors-and-programs
Contact: https://www.colum.edu/contact
Request for Information: https://apply.colum.edu/register/moreinfo
Phone: (312) 369-1000
Email: admissions@colum.edu

COST OF ATTENDANCE:

Tuition & Fees: $35,716 | **Additional Expenses:** $18,000
Total: $53,716

Financial Aid: https://www.colum.edu/columbia-central/where-to-start/index

ADDITIONAL INFORMATION:

Available Degree(s)
- BA Theatre Design and Technology
- BA Theatre, concentration: Stage Management

Freshman Portfolio Requirement
Portfolios are optional, however they are required for consideration for the Faculty Recognition Award. Submit via Columbia Connect Portal.

BA Theatre Design and Technology
- Resume of theatrical experiences
- 4-6 projects with written description of your role
  - Photographs or audio files of productions
  - Process examples, such as scenic sketches
  - Examples of drafting and construction skills

BA Theatre
- Resume of theatrical experiences and statement of goals
- 4-6 projects with written description of your role
  - Original scripts, annotated scripts or promptbooks, and 60-second video clips if you were the playwright, director, or stage manager

For more information, visit: https://www.colum.edu/admissions/additional-information/portfolio-and-audition-requirements

Scholarships Offered
Applicants that submit a portfolio are automatically considered for talent-based scholarships. Many internal scholarships are awarded to local high school graduates. For more information, visit: https://www.colum.edu/columbia-central/scholarships/index

Special Opportunities
Faculty-led study away opportunities for Theatre Design and Technology and Stage Management students include a 5-day New York Trip, International Theatre Workshop in London, International Theatre Workshop in Athens, and Bath Spa Textile Techniques Immersion.

Notable Alumni
- Anna D. Shapiro: Artistic Director at Steppenwolf Theatre
- Carter Howard: Acoustic and Vibration Consultant at The Papadimos Group
- Bob Teitel: Producer (*Men of Honor, Barbershop, Notorious*)

DEPAUL UNIVERSITY

Address: 2350 N. Racine Ave., Chicago, IL 60614
Website: https://theatre.depaul.edu/Pages/default.aspx
Contact: https://theatre.depaul.edu/about/Pages/contact-us.aspx
Request for Information: https://www.depaul.edu/admission-and-aid/Pages/request-info.aspx
Phone: (773) 325-7999
Email: theatreadmissions@depaul.edu

COST OF ATTENDANCE:

Tuition & Fees: $42,651 | **Additional Expenses:** $18,759
Total: $61,410

Financial Aid: https://www.depaul.edu/admission-and-aid/financial-aid/Pages/default.aspx

ADDITIONAL INFORMATION:

Available Degree(s)
- BFA Costume Design
- BFA Costume Technology
- BFA Lighting Design
- BFA Projection Design
- BFA Scene Design
- BFA Sound Design
- BFA Stage Management
- BFA Theatre Technology
- BFA Wig and Makeup Design & Technology

Freshman Portfolio Requirement
- All BFA programs require an interview and a resume
- All portfolios must include 10-20 pieces of work that relate to the chosen major
- For instance, the BFA in Costume Design encourages full costume designs or examples of sewing ability
- For the BFA in Stage Management, a writing sample, pre-screen, and an organized portfolio is required

For detailed information for each major's requirements, please click on your desired major and go to "How to Apply": https://theatre.depaul.edu/conservatory/undergraduate/Pages/default.aspx

Scholarships Offered
All applicants including international students are considered for the State Scholar Plus Scholarship (up to $100,000 over four years) and the DePaul Freshman Scholarships (award $15,000-$24,000 annually). Students admitted Early Action may earn donor-funded scholarships. For more information, visit: https://www.depaul.edu/admission-and-aid/Pages/scholarships.aspx

All students admitted to the Theatre School are awarded a Theatre School Scholarship ranging between $15,000 and $30,000.

Special Opportunities
DePaul offers a combined BFA/Master's program, allowing students to DePaul in five years. For more information, visit: https://theatre.depaul.edu/conservatory/undergraduate/Pages/combined-degree-programs.aspx

Notable Alumni
- Narda E. Alcorn: Broadway Stage Manager (*Choir Boy* and *The Iceman Cometh*)
- Erica Hemminger: Broadway Scenic Designer and Art Director For The Oscars
- Connor Wang: Broadway Sound Designer (*Hadestown* and *The Cher Show*)

ILLINOIS

INDIANA

IOWA

KANSAS

MICHIGAN

MINNESOTA

MISSOURI

NEBRASKA

NORTH DAKOTA

OHIO

SOUTH DAKOTA

WISCONSIN

MIDWEST

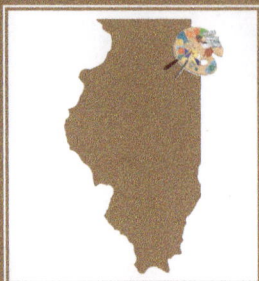

ILLINOIS

INDIANA

IOWA

KANSAS

MICHIGAN

MINNESOTA

MISSOURI

NEBRASKA

NORTH DAKOTA

OHIO

SOUTH DAKOTA

WISCONSIN

ND
MN
SD   WI
                    MI
NE   IA
            IL IN OH
    KS   MO

NORTHWESTERN UNIVERSITY

Address: 633 Clark St, Evanston, IL 60208
Website: https://communication.northwestern.edu/academic-programs/major-in-theatre/
Contact: https://www.communication.northwestern.edu/contact
Request for Information: https://ugadmission.northwestern.edu/register/request
Phone: (847) 491-3741
Email: dear-soc@northwestern.edu

COST OF ATTENDANCE:

Tuition & Fees: $60,768 | **Additional Expenses:** $23,070
Total: $83,838

Financial Aid: https://undergradaid.northwestern.edu/index.html

ADDITIONAL INFORMATION:

Available Degree(s)

- BA Theatre, area of study: Design & Stage Management

Freshman Portfolio Requirement

There is no portfolio requirement.

Scholarships Offered

The Northwestern University Scholarship ($250 to over $40,000 per year) is based on financial need after other forms of aid have been applied. The Karr Achievement Scholarship ($2,500 annually) is a merit-based scholarship. For more information, visit: https://undergradaid.northwestern.edu/types-of-aid/scholarships-grants/northwestern-scholarships.html

Special Opportunities

There is an Honors in Theatre program for students who demonstrate academic achievement and complete an Honors project.

Northwestern University offers a Major in Performance Studies, a Segal Design Certificate, a Minor in Sound Design, and a Minor in Music Technology. There is an Honors in Theatre program for students who demonstrate academic achievement and complete an Honors project.

Undergraduate courses for credit and on-campus certificate programs are open to high school students through the College Preparation Program. The Theatre Arts Division of the National High School Institute offers a 5-week Design/Technical program.

Theatre students may take advantage of study abroad opportunities with the British American Drama Academy in London, Goldsmiths, University of London, University of Glasgow, Prague Film School, and IFE's Paris Field Study & Internship Program.

Notable Alumni

- Barbara Gaines: Founder and Artistic Director at Chicago Shakespeare Theatre
- Martha Lavey: Artistic Director at Tony Award-Winning Steppenwolf Theatre Company
- John Musial: Founding Member of Tony Award-winning Lookingglass Theatre Company

UNIVERSITY OF ILLINOIS URBANA-CHAMPAIGN (UIUC)

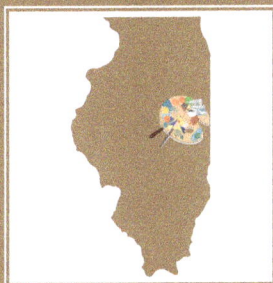

Address: 901 West Illinois Street, Urbana, IL 61801
Website: https://theatre.illinois.edu/training-programs/undergraduate-programs/
Contact: https://admissions.illinois.edu/contact
Request for Information: https://admissions.illinois.edu/request-more
Phone: (217) 333-0302
Email: admissions@illinois.edu

COST OF ATTENDANCE:

In-State Tuition & Fees: $16,866 | **Additional Expenses:** $16,194
Total: $33,060

Out-of-State Tuition & Fees: $34,316 |**Additional Expenses:** $16,534
Total: $50,850

Financial Aid: https://admissions.illinois.edu/Invest/financial-aid

ADDITIONAL INFORMATION:

Available Degree(s)
- BFA Theatre, concentrations:
  - Arts & Entertainment Technology
  - Costume Design & Technology
  - Lighting Design & Technology
  - Scenic Design
  - Scenic Technology
  - Sound Design & Technology
  - Stage Management

Freshman Portfolio Requirement
The 7 concentrations listed above are part of the Design, Technology, and Stage Management module. Applicants interested in any of these concentrations must submit a portfolio.

- Interview and resume required
- Sketches, draftings, photos of costumes, built scenes, etc.

For more information, visit: https://theatre.illinois.edu/apply/apply-undergraduate/portfolio-review-and-interview-for-design-technology-management/

Scholarships Offered
Both in-state and out-of-state applicants are eligible for various scholarships. Applicants are selected for College of Fine & Applied Arts talent-based awards during their audition, interview, and/or portfolio review. For more information, visit: https://admissions.illinois.edu/Invest/scholarships-all

Special Opportunities
The performance spaces at Krannert Center for the Performing Arts serve as labs for all theatre students. Students have access to the Krannert costume shop, the CU Community Fablab, and the wig and makeup studio. There are also two lighting laboratories and three professionally-equipped audio suites on campus.

Notable Alumni
- Kevin Adams (aka Kevin Shetterly): winner of 2002 Obie Award for Sustained Excellence of Lighting Design
- Lamar Farr: Music Producer, Audio Engineer and Sound Designer
- Rick Mireles: Stage Manager for Denver Center for the Performing Arts

ILLINOIS

INDIANA

IOWA

KANSAS

MICHIGAN

MINNESOTA

MISSOURI

NEBRASKA

NORTH DAKOTA

OHIO

SOUTH DAKOTA

WISCONSIN

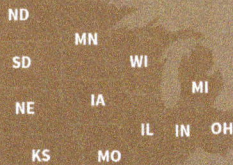

MIDWEST

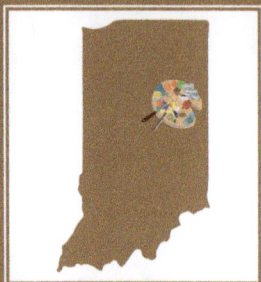

ILLINOIS

INDIANA

IOWA

KANSAS

MICHIGAN

MINNESOTA

MISSOURI

NEBRASKA

NORTH DAKOTA

OHIO

SOUTH DAKOTA

WISCONSIN

BALL STATE UNIVERSITY

Address: 2000 W University Ave, Muncie, IN 47306
Website: https://www.bsu.edu/academics/collegesanddepartments/
theatredance/what-we-offer
Contact: https://www.bsu.edu/admissions/undergraduate-
admissions/contact-us
Request for Information: https://admissions.bsu.edu/register/inquiry
Phone: (800) 482-4278
Email: askus@bsu.edu

COST OF ATTENDANCE:

In-State Tuition & Fees: $9,520 | **Additional Expenses:** $12,802
Total: $24,484

Out-of-State Tuition & Fees: $18,594 | **Additional Expenses:** $12,802
Total: $31,396

Financial Aid: https://www.bsu.edu/admissions/financial-aid-and-
scholarships

ADDITIONAL INFORMATION:

Available Degree(s)
- BA/BS in Theatre, Option: Design and Technology
- BFA in Theatre, Option: Design and Technology
- BA or BS in Theatre, Option: Directing and Stage Management
- BA or BS in Theatre, Option: Theatre Creation

Freshman Portfolio Requirement

All programs listed
- Resume
- Short statement of purpose
- Portfolio of works related to the option (e.g., sketches,
  renderings, prompt books, stage photographs, etc.)
- Interviews
- Required for the BFA in Theatre, Option: Design & Technology
- Encouraged for the other three programs

For more information, visit: https://www.bsu.edu/academics/
collegesanddepartments/theatredance/auditions-and-interviews

Scholarships Offered
The Department of Theatre and Dance offers merit-based
scholarships such as the University CFA Awards ($4,000 a year
for in-state students and $2,000 a year for out-of-state students).
For more information, visit: https://www.bsu.edu/academics/
collegesanddepartments/theatredance/scholarships

Special Opportunities
Students may study Theatre abroad at Worcester University, England,
Mainz University, Germany, University of Limerick, Ireland, Deakin
University, Australia, and through the The KIIS Prague Program.

Notable Alumni
- Brandon Reed: 2019 USITT Robert Cohen Sound Achievement
  Award winner and BroadwayWorld award nominee
- Christopher and Justin Swader: winners of 2011 KCACTF
  Barbizon Award for Scenic Design (*Angels in America, Part One:
  Millennium Approaches*)
- Kevin Depinet: Stage Designer (*Public Enemies*, the original
  Tony-award-winning *August: Osage County*, and *Of Mice and
  Men* on Broadway)

INDIANA UNIVERSITY AT BLOOMINGTON

Address: 107 S. Indiana Avenue, Bloomington, IN 47405
Website: https://theatre.indiana.edu/undergraduate/theatre-drama-ba/stage-management-ba.html
Contact: https://admissions.indiana.edu/contact/index.html
Request for Information: N/A
Phone: (812) 855-4848
Email: admissions@indiana.edu

COST OF ATTENDANCE:

In-State Tuition & Fees: $11,332 | **Additional Expenses:** $15,966
Total: $27,298

Out-of-State Tuition & Fees: $38,352 | **Additional Expenses:** $15,966
Total: $54,318

Financial Aid: https://admissions.indiana.edu/cost-financial-aid/financial-aid.html

ADDITIONAL INFORMATION:

Available Degree(s)
- BA Theatre: Design/Technology, Emphasis: Stage Management

Freshman Portfolio Requirement

There is no portfolio requirement.

Scholarships Offered
Indiana University Bloomington offers a variety of scholarships for in-state, out-of-state, and international students. Students applying before the early action deadline will receive consideration for IU Academic Scholarships ($1,000–$11,000) and for the invitation-only Selective Scholarship. For more information, visit: https://scholarships.indiana.edu/future-scholars/first-year-scholarships.html

There are also scholarships offered at the College of Arts and Sciences: https://theatre.indiana.edu/undergraduate/scholarships-awards/index.html

Special Opportunities
The O'Neill School of Public and Environmental Affairs offers a certificate in Arts Administration and a BA in Arts Management. Stage Management students may wish to complete an individualized degree through the Individualized Major Program to earn a unique degree and intern at a major arts organization. For more information, visit: https://imp.indiana.edu/

Among study abroad opportunities, theatre and drama students often pursue language study and other coursework through the Canterbury AY or Semester Program, the Costume and Character in London Theatre Summer Program, the London-IES Semester Program, and the Prague-CIEE Program.

Notable Alumni
- Tom Ridgely: Producing Artistic Director for Shakespeare Festival St. Louis
- Damont Martin: Artistic Director of Haven
- Emma Wesslund: Former Institutional Fundraising Coordinator at Shakespeare Theatre Company

ILLINOIS

INDIANA

IOWA

KANSAS

MICHIGAN

MINNESOTA

MISSOURI

NEBRASKA

NORTH DAKOTA

OHIO

SOUTH DAKOTA

WISCONSIN

MIDWEST

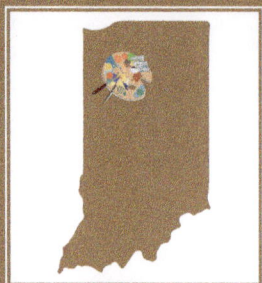

ILLINOIS

INDIANA

IOWA

KANSAS

MICHIGAN

MINNESOTA

MISSOURI

NEBRASKA

NORTH DAKOTA

OHIO

SOUTH DAKOTA

WISCONSIN

PURDUE UNIVERSITY

Address: Purdue University, West Lafayette, IN 47907
Website: https://cla.purdue.edu/academic/rueffschool/theatre/
academics/undergraduate/theatre.html
Contact: https://www.admissions.purdue.edu/contact/index.php
Request for Information: N/A
Phone: (765) 494-4600
Email: admissions@purdue.edu

COST OF ATTENDANCE:

In-State Tuition & Fees: $10,052 | **Additional Expenses:** $12,820
Total: $22,872

Out-of-State Tuition & Fees: $28,854 | **Additional Expenses:** $12,820
Total: $41,674

Financial Aid: https://www.purdue.edu/dfa/

ADDITIONAL INFORMATION:

Available Degree(s)

- BA Sound for the Performing Arts

Freshman Portfolio Requirement

There is no portfolio requirement.

Scholarships Offered

Purdue awards freshman scholarships based on academic merit
as well as financial need. The Trustees Scholarship awards $10,000
per year to in-state students and $16,000 per year to out-of-state
students. The Presidential Scholarship awards $4,000 per year to
in-state students and $10,000 per year to out-of-state students.
For more information, visit: https://www.admissions.purdue.edu/
costsandfinaid/freshman.php

There are also scholarships available to Theatre majors that are
selected by The Scholarship Committee or faculty and staff of
the Department of Theatre: https://cla.purdue.edu/academic/
rueffschool/theatre/academics/scholarships.html

Special Opportunities

Students may apply for the 5-year BS/MS degree in Computer
Graphics Technology. For more information, visit: https://polytechnic.
purdue.edu/departments/computer-graphics-technology/three-plus-
two

Purdue Study Abroad offers two programs of theatre study in England
through University of Coventry and University of Kent at Canterbury.
For more information, visit: https://cla.purdue.edu/academic/
rueffschool/theatre/documents/Study%20Abroad%20in%20England.
pdf

Notable Alumni

- Rob James: Consultant at Threshold Acoustics
- Andrew Hanson: Audio/Stage Technician at 2K Games
- Kirk Powell: Design Engineer managing audio operation for the
  Super Bowl

UNIVERSITY OF EVANSVILLE

Address: 1800 Lincoln Ave, Evansville, IN 47722
Website: https://www.evansville.edu/majors/theatre/degrees.cfm
Contact: https://www.evansville.edu/contact/
Request for Information: https://www.evansville.edu/admission/requestmore.cfm
Phone: (833) 232-6223
Email: uerelations@evansville.edu

COST OF ATTENDANCE:

Tuition & Fees: $41,336 | **Additional Expenses:** $17,110
Total: $58,446

Financial Aid: https://www.evansville.edu/student-financial-services/

ADDITIONAL INFORMATION:

Available Degree(s)
- BFA in Theatre Design and Technology
- BS in Theatre Design and Technology
- BS in Stage Management
- BS in Theatre Management

Freshman Portfolio Requirement
- Interview required
- Applicants to all four programs listed must undergo a portfolio review
- Resume required
- Photographs, prompt-scripts, drawings of productions all encouraged
- Theatre management applicants must also submit writing samples

For more information, visit: https://www.evansville.edu/majors/theatre/auditions.cfm

Scholarships Offered
Any remaining gap between a student's UE Scholarships, Indiana State Grant Funding, and Federal Grant Funding and full-time tuition and full-time fees will be covered through an Aces Opportunity Grant. Merit-based scholarships include Presidential Scholarship ($21,000 at minimum). For more information, visit: https://www.evansville.edu/student-financial-services/scholarships-overview.cfm

Special Opportunities
At Harlaxton College, UE's study abroad center in England, Theatre students may take Introduction to Theatre and Period Styles in Theatre: Costume History in the summer or British Studies: Literary Perspectives, Independent Study in British Theatre, and Shakespeare in a fall or spring semester. For more information, visit: https://www.evansville.edu/studyabroad/

Notable Alumni
- Leslie Oberhausen: Stage Manager at the Louisville Ballet
- Joshua Marsh: Costume Designer (*Girls, Orange Is the New Black*)
- Holli Campbell: Broadway Company Manager

ILLINOIS

INDIANA

IOWA

KANSAS

MICHIGAN

MINNESOTA

MISSOURI

NEBRASKA

NORTH DAKOTA

OHIO

SOUTH DAKOTA

WISCONSIN

MIDWEST

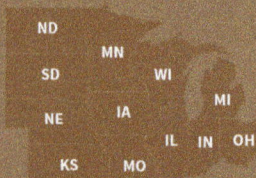

WICHITA STATE UNIVERSITY

Address: 1845 Fairmount St, Wichita, KS 67260
Website: https://www.wichita.edu/academics/fine_arts/spa/3_
THEATRE/index.php
Contact: https://www.wichita.edu/academics/academic_affairs/
Contact.php
Request for Information: https://www.wichita.edu/about/rfi_
splitter_lp.php
Phone: (316) 978-3010
Email: uerelations@evansville.edu

COST OF ATTENDANCE:

In-State Tuition & Fees: $8,103 | **Additional Expenses:** $17,260
Total: $25,363

Out-of-State Tuition & Fees: $16,973 | **Additional Expenses:** $17,260
Total: $34,233

Financial Aid: https://www.wichita.edu/administration/financial_aid/

ADDITIONAL INFORMATION:

Available Degree(s)
- BFA Theatre Design & Technology, specializations:
  o Lighting Design
  o Sound Design
  o Costume Design
  o Set Design
  o Scenic Technology

Freshman Portfolio Requirement
- Interview not required, but strongly encouraged
- Technical resume
- Submit drawings, photos of work, renderings, etc.

For more information, visit: https://www.wichita.edu/academics/
fine_arts/spa/3_THEATRE/AuditionsPROGRAMtheatre.php

Scholarships Offered
Wichita State University offers tuition discounts, financial aids,
and scholarships. Both in-state students and out-of-state students
are eligible for The Freshmen Merit Scholarship ($1,000 - $4,000 a
year and $2,500 - $6,000 a year respectively). WSU's National Merit
Scholarships (up to $50,000 over four years) are open to National
Merit Finalists and National Hispanic Recognition Finalists. The
Global Select Scholarships ($500 - $2,500 a year) are awarded to
international students based on their performance at WSU. For
more information, visit: https://www.wichita.edu/administration/
financial_aid/scholarships/

Special Opportunities
The College of Fine Arts participates in WSU's cooperative education
internship program, which aims to provide paid employment
experiences that complement the curriculum.

The Theatre Program offers a Certificate in Stage Management.

Notable Alumni
- Sai Baig Powers: Stage Manager at Phoenix Theatre Cookie
  Company
- Kate Snodgrass: Artistic Director at Boston Playwrights Theatre;
  graduate of London Academy of Music and Dramatic Art
- Paul Colella: Vice President at McClelland Sound

UNIVERSITY OF MICHIGAN

Address: 500 S. State St., Ann Arbor, MI 48109
Website: https://smtd.umich.edu/programs-degrees/degree-programs/undergraduate/theatre-drama/bachelor-of-fine-arts-in-design-production/
Contact: https://smtd.umich.edu/about/contact-us/
Request for Information: N/A
Phone: (734) 764-0593
Email: smtd.admissions@umich.edu

COST OF ATTENDANCE:

In-State Tuition & Fees: $18,208 | **Additional Expenses:** $16,094
Total: $34,302

Out-of-State Tuition & Fees: $56,962 | **Additional Expenses:** $16,094
Total: $73,056

Financial Aid: https://finaid.umich.edu/

ADDITIONAL INFORMATION:

Available Degree(s)
- BFA Design & Production
- BFA Performing Arts Technology

Freshman Portfolio Requirement
- Interview required, virtually or in-person
- Submit portfolio via University of Michigan portal
- Personal statement
- Portfolio of works

For more information, visit: https://smtd.umich.edu/admissions/undergraduate-admissions/auditions-interviews/

Scholarships Offered
University of Michigan offers several scholarships for incoming students. One of them is the Stamps Scholars Program, a prestigious merit-based program that offers the full cost of attendance. The HAIL Scholarship is an invitational award that covers four years of tuition and fees for low-income, high achieving Michigan students. Many scholarships are need-based, although some are merit-based as well. For more information, visit: https://finaid.umich.edu/scholarships-at-u-m/

The School of Music, Theatre & Dance offers merit-based scholarships to students. For more information, visit: https://smtd.umich.edu/admissions/undergraduate-admissions/cost-scholarships-financial-aid/

Special Opportunities
The School of Music, Theatre & Dance also offers a BS in Sound Engineering and a minor in Performing Arts Management and Entrepreneurship.

Study away opportunities include exchange programs in Conservatoire de Paris, France, Hochschule fur Musik, Karlsruhe, Germany, Trinity Laban Conservatoire, London, England, and Zurich University of the Arts in Zurich, Switzerland.

Notable Alumni
- Tobin Ost: nominee of Tony Award for Best Scenic Design in a Musical
- Jean-Luc DeLadurantaye: Costume Designer (*Jagged Little Pill at A.R.T, Broadway: Gettin' the Band Back Together*)
- Mitch Hodges: Stage Manager (*The Phantom of the Opera, North America Tour*)

ILLINOIS

INDIANA

IOWA

KANSAS

MICHIGAN

MINNESOTA

MISSOURI

NEBRASKA

NORTH DAKOTA

OHIO

SOUTH DAKOTA

WISCONSIN

MIDWEST

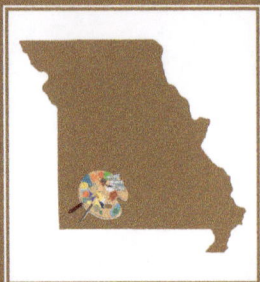

ILLINOIS

INDIANA

IOWA

KANSAS

MICHIGAN

MINNESOTA

MISSOURI

NEBRASKA

NORTH DAKOTA

OHIO

SOUTH DAKOTA

WISCONSIN

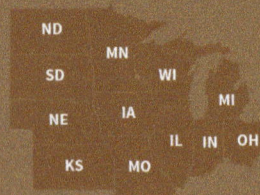

MISSOURI STATE UNIVERSITY

Address: 901 S National Ave, Springfield, MO 65897
Website: https://theatreanddance.missouristate.edu/design-technology.htm
Contact: https://theatreanddance.missouristate.edu/Contact.aspx
Request for Information: https://www.missouristate.edu/futurestudents/request-info.htm
Phone: (417) 836-4400
Email: TheatreAndDance@MissouriState.edu

COST OF ATTENDANCE:

In-State Tuition & Fees: $8,294 | **Additional Expenses:** $14,874
Total: $23,168

Out-of-State Tuition & Fees: $16,498 | **Additional Expenses:** $14,874
Total: $31,372

Financial Aid: https://www.missouristate.edu/financialaid/

ADDITIONAL INFORMATION:

Available Degree(s)
- BFA Design, Technology, and Stage Management

Freshman Portfolio Requirement
- Interview required if applicant wants to be considered for a scholarship
- Bring resume and portfolio

Please note that you must apply as a pre-admit major into this program. Once you pass the BFA review during your first year, you are then officially admitted into the program. For more information, visit: https://theatreanddance.missouristate.edu/Undergraduate/Audition.htm

Scholarships Offered
Missouri State University funds automatic scholarships based on students' GPA and standardized test score as well as competitive scholarships including the Presidential Scholarship (up to $60,000 over four years) and the Inclusive Excellence Scholarship (up to $21,000 over four years). For more information, visit: https://www.missouristate.edu/FinancialAid/Scholarships/Freshman.htm

The theatre and dance department awards sixteen $2,000 activity scholarships as recommended by the faculty and six $2,000 scholarships associated with the department's student theatre troupe, In-School Players, are assigned via an audition process. Numerous other scholarships are awarded with various criteria. For more information, visit: https://theatreanddance.missouristate.edu/Scholarships.htm

Special Opportunities
The BFA program offers a three-year transfer plan and a three-year plus one semester degree plan.

Every other year, the department sponsors a group trip to Toronto to train and get certified with Fight Directors Canada's Stage Combat Certification Program. Theatre students may study away with the Theatre Academy London (TAL) in England.

Notable Alumni
- Alice Bristow: Costume Designer and Professor at Berry College
- Zachary Quarles: Video Game Sound Designer (*DOOM, Quake,* and *Killer Instinct*)
- Amber Hensley: Stage Manager at Norwegian Cruise Line Holdings

UNIVERSITY OF MISSOURI

Address: University of Missouri, Columbia, MO 65211
Website: https://majors.missouri.edu/theatre-design-technical-ba/
Contact: https://admissions.missouri.edu/contact/
Request for Information: https://admissions.missouri.edu/contact/
Phone: (573) 882-7786
Email: askmizzou@missouri.edu

COST OF ATTENDANCE:

In-State Tuition & Fees: $13,128 | **Additional Expenses:** $10,964
Total: $24,092

Out-of-State Tuition & Fees: $31,734 | **Additional Expenses:** $10,964
Total: $42,698

Financial Aid: https://admissions.missouri.edu/financial-aid/

ADDITIONAL INFORMATION:

Available Degree(s)
- BA in Theatre, concentration: Design/Technical

Freshman Portfolio Requirement
There is no portfolio requirement.

Scholarships Offered
University of Missouri offers automatic scholarships to in-state students, out-of-state students, and international students. Applicants who apply test-optional and do not have official test scores are reviewed holistically for scholarships. Competitive awards include the Stamps Scholars Award (full scholarship). For more information, visit: https://admissions.missouri.edu/scholarships/

The Theatre Department established the Dan Springer Memorial Fund, which provides scholarships to Theatre students studying the technical arts involved in performance. There are also department-level scholarships awarded to current students. For more information, visit: https://theatre.missouri.edu/scholarships-and-giving

Special Opportunities
MU's principal theatre, The Rhynsburger Theatre, houses a variety of light and sound equipment and control systems and a state-of-the-art professional computer graphics lab. Students also have access to a costume shop and a scene shop.

Students may study abroad in Lancaster University and University of East Anglia in England.

Notable Alumni
- Rhonda Weller-Stilson: Costume and Scenic Designer; professor at Southeast Missouri State University
- Gary Mickelson: Broadway Stage Manager (*Gypsy, Company*, and *Chita Rivera: The Dancer's Life*)
- Clista Jarrett: Stage Manager and Props Master

ILLINOIS

INDIANA

IOWA

KANSAS

MICHIGAN

MINNESOTA

MISSOURI

NEBRASKA

NORTH DAKOTA

OHIO

SOUTH DAKOTA

WISCONSIN

MIDWEST

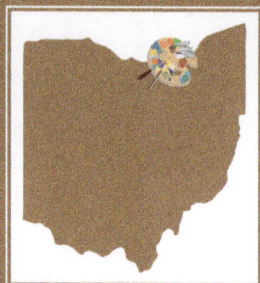

ILLINOIS

INDIANA

IOWA

KANSAS

MICHIGAN

MINNESOTA

MISSOURI

NEBRASKA

NORTH DAKOTA

OHIO

SOUTH DAKOTA

WISCONSIN

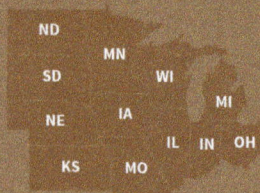

BALDWIN WALLACE UNIVERSITY

Address: 275 Eastland Rd, Berea, OH 44017
Website: https://www.bw.edu/academics/undergraduate/theatre-design-technical/
Contact: https://www.bw.edu/admission/counselors/
Request for Information: https://www.bw.edu/admission/request-information/
Phone: (440) 826-2222
Email: admission@bw.edu

COST OF ATTENDANCE:

Tuition & Fees: $35,366 | **Additional Expenses:** $13,024
Total: $48,390

Financial Aid: https://www.bw.edu/undergraduate-admission/first-year/tuition/

ADDITIONAL INFORMATION:

Available Degree(s)

- BA Theatre, concentrations:
  o Design & Technical
  o Stage Management

Freshman Portfolio Requirement

There is no portfolio requirement. Interviews are optional, although encouraged.

Scholarships Offered

First-year applicants are automatically considered for merit scholarships ($12,000 to $21,000 a year) based on their cumulative weighted high school GPA. Baldwin Wallace University also offers numerous special awards. For more information, visit: https://www.bw.edu/undergraduate-admission/first-year/tuition/

Special Opportunities

Students have access to the Kleist Center for Art & Drama, which houses the Mainstage Theatre and the Black Box Theatre. With a new lighting system installed by ETC and over 200 dimmers, lights are operated on an Emphasis board including a WYSIWYG program in the Mainstage Theatre. The Black Box Theatre boasts a new Strand Century Lighting system with a 520 series light board.

Theatre students can take a three-week faculty-led British theatre course in English including a nine-day trip to London. BW also offers study abroad opportunities such as Explore Europe as well as Theatre in London.

Notable Alumni

- Nicholas Moertl: Technical Designer (Lady Gaga's Super Bowl LI halftime show)
- Dane Urban: Stage Manager at Manhattan School of Music
- Steven Caple Jr.: Film Producer, Director, and Screenwriter (*The Land, Creed II*, and *A Different Tree*)

KENT STATE UNIVERSITY

Address: 1325 Theatre Drive, Kent, OH 44242
Website: https://www.kent.edu/theatredance/bachelor-fine-arts-theatre-design-technology-and-production
Contact: https://www.kent.edu/theatredance/contact-us
Request for Information: https://ksu.secure.force.com/form/?formid=217802
Phone: (330) 672-2082
Email: theatre@kent.edu

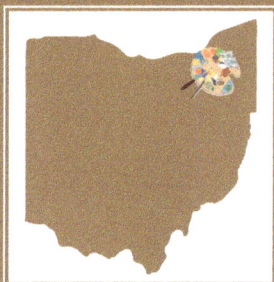

COST OF ATTENDANCE:

In-State Tuition & Fees: $11,923 | **Additional Expenses:** $17,745
Total: $29,668

Out-of-State Tuition & Fees: $20,799 | **Additional Expenses:** $17,745
Total: $38,544

Financial Aid: https://www.kent.edu/financialaid

ADDITIONAL INFORMATION:

Available Degree(s)

- BFA Design Technology & Production

Freshman Portfolio Requirement

There is no portfolio requirement.

Scholarships Offered

Both in-state and out-of-state applicants are eligible for merit-based awards, including the President's Achievement Award ($1,000 - $4,000 for in-state students and $4,000-$12,500 for out-of-state students), the Honors Distinction Award ($2,000), and the Founders Scholarship ($1,000-$2,000). For more information, visit: https://www.kent.edu/scholarships

Special Opportunities

Porthouse Theatre, Kent State University's summer professional theatre, hosts summer programs for high school students, college students, and international students.

The School of Theatre and Dance supports students' participation in the Edinburgh Festival Fringe in Edinburgh, Scotland. Students can also study theatre at the Accademia dell'Arte in Italy and the University of Roehampton through ISEP Direct programs.

Notable Alumni

- Cyndi Hoffman: Pyrotechnician and Lighting Technician at Texas Musical Drama and Holland America Cruise (*Alaska in Concert*)
- DH Taylor: Stage and Event Manager; Theatre Technician (UK National Tour of *Count Arthur Strong*)
- Kathleen Kovarik: Costume Designer at Playhouse on the Square

ILLINOIS

INDIANA

IOWA

KANSAS

MICHIGAN

MINNESOTA

MISSOURI

NEBRASKA

NORTH DAKOTA

OHIO

SOUTH DAKOTA

WISCONSIN

MIDWEST

UNIVERSITY OF CINCINNATI

Address: 2600 Clifton Ave, Cincinnati, OH 45221
Website: https://ccm.uc.edu/areas-of-study/academic-units/theatre-design-production.html
Contact: https://admissions.uc.edu/contact.html
Request for Information: https://admissions.uc.edu/contact/request-info.html
Phone: (513) 556-6000
Email: admissions@uc.edu

COST OF ATTENDANCE:

In-State Tuition & Fees: $12,598 | **Additional Expenses:** $16,510
Total: $29,108

Out-of-State Tuition & Fees: $27,932 | **Additional Expenses:** $11,874
Total: $44,442

Financial Aid: https://financialaid.uc.edu/

ADDITIONAL INFORMATION:

Available Degree(s)
- BFA in Theatre Design and Production, concentrations:
  o Costume Design and Technology
  o Lighting Design and Technology
  o Sound Design
  o Stage Design, Props and Scenic Art
  o Stage Management
  o Technical Production

Freshman Portfolio Requirement
- Interview required
- Resume, 3 letters of recommendation, and questionnaire
- 500-word applicant statement
- Portfolio (artistic and theatrical work)

For more information, visit: https://ccm.uc.edu/areas-of-study/academic-units/theatre-design-production.html

Scholarships Offered
Applicants are automatically reviewed for merit-based scholarships at the University of Cincinnati. The University of Cincinnati Global Scholarship ($1,000 to $15,000 each year) is exclusively for international applicants. For more information, visit: https://www.kent.edu/scholarships

The College-Conservatory of Music offers talent-based scholarships as well as academic scholarships. For more information, visit: https://ccm.uc.edu/admissions-and-aid/financial-aid.html

Special Opportunities
CCM's Corbett Center for the Performing Arts houses a scene shop, a costume shop, wig, make-up and prosthetics studios, a design/drafting studio, a light lab, sound design studios, and CAD drafting stations.

Notable Alumni
- Cara Hannah Sullivan: winner of Emmy Award for Outstanding Hairstyling For A Multi-Camera Series Or Special 2012-2016, winner of Emmy Award for Outstanding Contemporary Hairstyling For A Variety, Nonfiction Or Reality Program 2021
- Debbie Denise: Executive Vice President of production infrastructure at Sony Pictures Imageworks
- Kevin McCollum: Tony Award-winning Broadway Producer (*Rent, Avenue Q*, and *Motown: The Musical*)

UNIVERSITY OF WISCONSIN

Address: 821 University Ave., 6173 Vilas Hall, Madison, WI 53706
Website: https://theatre.wisc.edu/academics/bachelor-of-science-in-theatre-and-drama/
Contact: https://theatre.wisc.edu/contact/
Request for Information: https://uwmadison.secure.force.com/admissions/UW_RFI_Form_Generic
Phone: (608) 263-2329
Email: uwtheatre@theatre.wisc.edu

COST OF ATTENDANCE:

In-State Tuition & Fees: $10,766 | **Additional Expenses:** $16,764
Total: $27,530

Out-of-State Tuition & Fees: $38,654 | **Additional Expenses:** $17,234
Total: $55,888

MN Resident Tuition & Fees: $14,812 | **Additional Expenses:** $17,044
Total: $31,856

Financial Aid: https://financialaid.wisc.edu/

ADDITIONAL INFORMATION:

Available Degree(s)
- BS Theatre and Drama, informal emphases:
  - o Design
  - o Stage Management
  - o Theatre Technology

Freshman Portfolio Requirement
There is no portfolio requirement.

Scholarships Offered
Theatre-specific scholarships are available. Students are encouraged to browse through current offerings. For more information, visit: https://theatre.wisc.edu/scholarships/

The University of Wisconsin also offers various institutional awards. Students are encouraged to browse through the Wisconsin Scholarship Hub (WiSH): https://wisc.academicworks.com/

Special Opportunities
The UW-Madison Department of Theatre and Drama produces many productions that students may audition for. For more information, visit: https://theatre.wisc.edu/productions-and-tickets/student-opportunities/

Theatre students may study abroad through the UW Global Launch in London and UW in London programs.

Notable Alumni
- Carol Helen Beule: Emmy Award–winning Costume Designer (*Alice's Adventures in Wonderland*)
- Rocco Landesman: Broadway Producer and Former Chair of National Endowment for the Arts
- Lisa Heller: Executive Vice President of HBO documentary and family programming

ILLINOIS

INDIANA

IOWA

KANSAS

MICHIGAN

MINNESOTA

MISSOURI

NEBRASKA

NORTH DAKOTA

OHIO

SOUTH DAKOTA

WISCONSIN

MIDWEST

ALABAMA

ARKANSAS

DELAWARE

DISTRICT OF
COLUMBIA

FLORIDA

GEORGIA

KENTUCKY

LOUISIANA

MARYLAND

MISSISSIPPI

NORTH CAROLINA

OKLAHOMA

SOUTH CAROLINA

TENNESSEE

TEXAS

VIRGINIA

WEST VIRGINIA

CHAPTER 15

REGION THREE

SOUTH

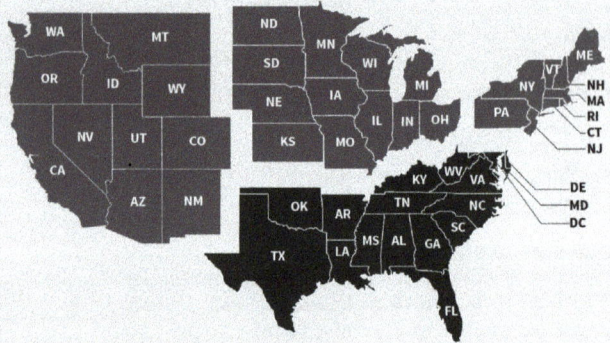

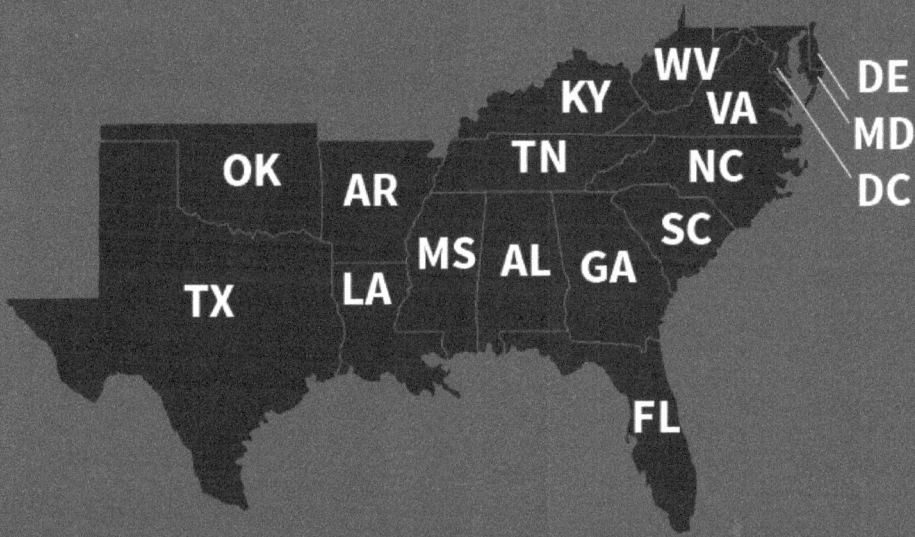

13 Programs | 16 States

1. AL – Auburn University
2. GA – Savannah College of Art and Design (SCAD)
3. LA – Tulane University
4. NC – Catawba College
5. NC – Elon University
6. NC – University of North Carolina School of the Arts
7. OK – Oklahoma City University
8. OK – University of Oklahoma
9. TN – Belmont University
10. TX – Baylor University
11. TX – Texas Christian University (TCU)
12. VA – Shenandoah University
13. VA – Virginia Commonwealth University (VCU)

COSTUME DESIGN & TECHNICAL THEATRE SCHOOLS

School	Avg. GPA, SAT Evidence-Based Reading Writing (ERW), SAT Math (M), and ACT Composite (C) Early Decision (ED): Yes/No	Admission Statistics	Program(s)	Portfolio, Interview, and/ or Audition Required (Req.)
Auburn University Auburn University, Auburn, AL 36849	GPA: 3.97 SAT (ERW): 590-650 SAT (M): 570-670 ACT (C): 25-31 ED: No	Admit Rate: 85% Undergrad Enrollment: 24,505 Total Enrollment: 30,737	BFA Theatre Management BFA Design and Technology Degrees Awarded in the Program(s) (2020): 19	Portfolio: Not req. Interview: Not req. Audition: Not req.
Savannah College of Art and Design (SCAD) 516 Drayton St, Savannah, GA 31401	GPA: 3.6 SAT (ERW): 540-640 SAT (M): 500-600 ACT (C): 20-27 ED: No	Admit Rate: 78% Undergrad Enrollment: 11,679 Total Enrollment: 14,265	BFA Production Design, concentrations: Costume Design Lighting Design Set Design and Art Direction Degrees Awarded in the Program(s) (2020): 47	Portfolio: Not req. Interview: Not req. Audition: Not req.
Tulane University 215 McWilliams Hall New Orleans, Louisiana 70118	GPA: 3.55 SAT (ERW): 650-730 SAT (M): 690-770 ACT (C): 30-33 ED: Yes	Admit Rate: 11% Undergrad Enrollment: 8,537 Total Enrollment: 13,927	BFA Theatre: Design/ Production Emphasis BA Theatre: Design/ Technology Emphasis Degrees Awarded in the Program(s) (2020): 1	Portfolio: Not req. Interview: Not req. Audition: Not req.

COSTUME DESIGN & TECHNICAL THEATRE SCHOOLS

School	Avg. GPA, SAT Evidence-Based Reading Writing (ERW), SAT Math (M), and ACT Composite (C) Early Decision (ED): Yes/No	Admission Statistics	Program(s)	Portfolio, Interview, and/ or Audition Required (Req.)
Catawba College 2300 W Innes St, Salisbury, NC 28144	GPA: 3.59 SAT (ERW): 470-570 SAT (M): 470-570 ACT (C): 17-22 ED: No	Admit Rate: 52% Undergrad Enrollment: 1,340 Total Enrollment: 1,371	BFA Theatre Arts, concentration: Design and Production Degrees Awarded in the Program(s) (2020): N/A	Portfolio: Not req. Interview: Not req. Audition: Not req.
Elon University 100 Campus Drive, Elon, NC 27244	GPA: 4.04 SAT (ERW): 580-660 SAT (M): 560-660 ACT (C): 25-30 ED: Yes	Admit Rate: 72% Undergrad Enrollment: 6,291 Total Enrollment: 7,117	BA Theatrical Design & Technology Degrees Awarded in the Program(s) (2020): 12	Portfolio: Not req. Interview: Not req. Audition: Not req.

SOUTH

COSTUME DESIGN &
TECHNICAL THEATRE SCHOOLS

School	Avg. GPA, SAT Evidence-Based Reading Writing (ERW), SAT Math (M), and ACT Composite (C) Early Decision (ED): Yes/No	Admission Statistics	Program(s)	Portfolio, Interview, and/ or Audition Required (Req.)
University of North Carolina School of the Arts 1533 S Main St, Winston-Salem, NC 27127	GPA: 3.69 SAT (ERW): 590-670 SAT (M): 530-640 ACT (C): 22-29 ED: No	Admit Rate: 36% Undergrad Enrollment: 920 Total Enrollment: 1,070	BFA Costume Design & Technology BFA Lighting BFA Scene Design BFA Scene Painting BFA Scenic Technology BFA Sound Design BFA Stage Management BFA Stage Properties BFA Wig & Makeup Design Degrees Awarded in the Program(s) (2020): 67	Portfolio: Req. Interview: Req. for certain programs Audition: Not req.

School	Avg. GPA, SAT Evidence-Based Reading Writing (ERW), SAT Math (M), and ACT Composite (C) Early Decision (ED): Yes/No	Admission Statistics	Program(s)	Portfolio, Interview, and/or Audition Required (Req.)
Oklahoma City University 2501 N. Blackwelder, Oklahoma City, OK 73106	GPA: N/A SAT (ERW): 550-650 SAT (M): 530-610 ACT (C): 22-29 ED: No	Admit Rate: 73% Undergrad Enrollment: 1,527 Total Enrollment: 2,617	BFA Design & Production, emphases: Costume Design & Technology Stage & Production Management Lighting Design Scenic Design Props Design and Fabrication Sound Design Degrees Awarded in the Program(s) (2020): 10	Portfolio: Req. Interview: Req. Audition: Not req.

SOUTH

COSTUME DESIGN & TECHNICAL THEATRE SCHOOLS

School	Avg. GPA, SAT Evidence-Based Reading Writing (ERW), SAT Math (M), and ACT Composite (C) Early Decision (ED): Yes/No	Admission Statistics	Program(s)	Portfolio, Interview, and/or Audition Required (Req.)
University of Oklahoma 660 Parrington Oval, Norman, OK 73019	GPA: 3.63 SAT (ERW): 560-650 SAT (M): 540-650 ACT (C): 23-29 ED: No	Admit Rate: 83% Undergrad Enrollment: 21,383 Total Enrollment: 27,772	BFA Drama, emphasis: Design, tracks: Scenic Design Costume Design Lighting Design Sound Design BFA Theatre, emphasis: Stage Management Degrees Awarded in the Program(s) (2020): N/A	Portfolio: Req. Interview: Req. Audition: Not req.
Belmont University 1900 Belmont Blvd, Nashville, TN 37212	GPA: 3.83 SAT (ERW): 580-660 SAT (M): 540-640 ACT (C): 23-30 ED: No	Admit Rate: 83% Undergrad Enrollment: 6,631 Total Enrollment: 8,204	BFA Theatre, concentration: Production Design Degrees Awarded in the Program(s) (2020): 3	Portfolio: Req. Interview: Not req. Audition: Not req.

School	Avg. GPA, SAT Evidence-Based Reading Writing (ERW), SAT Math (M), and ACT Composite (C) Early Decision (ED): Yes/No	Admission Statistics	Program(s)	Portfolio, Interview, and/or Audition Required (Req.)
Baylor University 1311 S 5th St, Waco, TX 76706	GPA: N/A SAT (ERW): 600-680 SAT (M): 590-680 ACT (C): 26-31 ED: Yes	Admit Rate: 68% Undergrad Enrollment: 14,399 Total Enrollment: 19,297	BFA Theatre Design and Technology, specializations: Costume and Makeup Design Lighting Design Scenic Design & Technology Sound & Media Design Stage Management Degrees Awarded in the Program(s) (2020): 3	Portfolio: Req. Interview: Req. Audition: Not req.
Texas Christian University (TCU) 2800 South University Drive Fort Worth, Texas 76109	GPA: N/A SAT (ERW): 560-660 SAT (M): 550-660 ACT (C): 25-31 ED: No	Admit Rate: 48% Undergrad Enrollment: 9,704 Total Enrollment: 11,379	BFA Theatre, emphasis: Design & Technology Degrees Awarded in the Program(s) (2020): 1	Portfolio: Req. Interview: Req. Audition: Not req.

SOUTH

COSTUME DESIGN & TECHNICAL THEATRE SCHOOLS

School	Avg. GPA, SAT Evidence-Based Reading Writing (ERW), SAT Math (M), and ACT Composite (C) Early Decision (ED): Yes/No	Admission Statistics	Program(s)	Portfolio, Interview, and/or Audition Required (Req.)
Shenandoah University 1460 University Dr, Winchester, VA 22601	GPA: 3.55 SAT (ERW): 510-630 SAT (M): 500-600 ACT (C): 19-26 ED: No	Admit Rate: 74% Undergrad Enrollment: 2,267 Total Enrollment: 4,174	BFA Theatre Design & Production, emphases: Costume Design Lighting Design Scenic Design Sound Design and Reinforcement Stage Management Technical Production Degrees Awarded in the Program(s) (2020): 3	Portfolio: Req. Interview: Req. Audition: Not req.
Virginia Commonwealth University (VCU) Virginia Commonwealth University, Richmond, VA 23284	GPA: 3.72 SAT (ERW): 540-640 SAT (M): 520-610 ACT (C): 21-28 ED: No	Admit Rate: 91% Undergrad Enrollment: 21,943 Total Enrollment: 29,070	BFA Theatre concentrations: Costume Design Lighting Design Scenic Design Stage Management Degrees Awarded in the Program(s) (2020): 36	Portfolio: Req. Interview: Req. Audition: Not req.

ALABAMA

ARKANSAS

DELAWARE

DISTRICT OF COLUMBIA

FLORIDA

GEORGIA

KENTUCKY

LOUISIANA

MARYLAND

MISSISSIPPI

NORTH CAROLINA

OKLAHOMA

SOUTH CAROLINA

TENNESSEE

TEXAS

VIRGINIA

WEST VIRGINIA

AUBURN UNIVERSITY

Address: Auburn University, Auburn, AL 36849
Website: https://cla.auburn.edu/theatre/academics/bfa-design-tech/
Contact: http://www.auburn.edu/enrollment/contact_us.php
Request for Information: https://apply.auburn.edu/register/inquiryform
Phone: (334) 844-4084
Email: ulricpv@auburn.edu

COST OF ATTENDANCE:

In-State Tuition & Fees: $11,796 | **Additional Expenses:** $21,648
Total: $33,444

Out-of-State Tuition & Fees: $31,956 | **Additional Expenses:** $21,648
Total: $53,604

Financial Aid: http://www.auburn.edu/administration/business-finance/finaid/

ADDITIONAL INFORMATION:

Available Degree(s)

- BFA Theatre Management
- BFA Design and Technology

Freshman Portfolio Requirement

There is no portfolio requirement for incoming freshmen. Interested BFA students enter as BA students and only gain acceptance to the BFA program after a successful portfolio review towards the end of their second year.

Scholarships Offered

Applicants are eligible for merit-based and achievement scholarships. Non-resident scholarships are up to $16,500 and resident scholarships go up to $10,500. Auburn University also awards general scholarships and department scholarships. For more information, visit: http://www.auburn.edu/scholarship/index.php#UndergraduateScholarships

Special Opportunities

The Telfair Peet Theatre houses multi-story costume and scenery shops and a black box theatre with a state-of-the-art digital lighting system.

Every year, the Department of Theatre hosts a Scholarship Day in late October.

Dedicated to the creation of original works of theatre that explore issues of diversity, the Mosaic Theatre Company (MTC) recruits members from the Auburn University student body to develop new materials and strengthen their theatrical skills. For more information, visit: https://cla.auburn.edu/theatre/ensembles/mosaic/

Theatre students can take advantage of study abroad programs including summer seminars in Galway, Ireland, Barcelona, and Spain.

SAVANNAH COLLEGE OF ART & DESIGN (SCAD)

Address: 342 Bull St., Savannah, GA 31401
Website: https://www.scad.edu/academics/programs/production-design
Contact: https://www.scad.edu/about/contact
Request for Information: https://admission.scad.edu/forms/reqInfo/rfi2
Phone: (912) 525-5100
Email: contact@scad.edu
Other locations: Atlanta, GA

COST OF ATTENDANCE:

Tuition & Fees: $38,340 | **Additional Expenses:** $15,269
Total: $53,609

Financial Aid: https://www.scad.edu/admission/financial-aid-and-scholarships

ADDITIONAL INFORMATION:

Available Degree(s)

- BFA Production Design, concentrations:
  - Costume Design
  - Lighting Design
  - Set Design and Art Direction

Freshman Portfolio Requirement
Portfolios are optional. However, they are required for achievement honors scholarship consideration.

- Submit via SlideRoom
- Portfolio may fall under any of the categories: Business and Marketing, Visual Arts, Time-based Media, Visual and Time-based Media, Writing, or Performing Arts
- Applicants are encouraged to submit a portfolio related to their major of choice
- For visual arts portfolios, applicants must submit 10-20 visual artworks and/or 3D renderingsAll work submitted must be original in concept and fabrication

For more information, visit: https://www.scad.edu/admission/portfolio-and-writing-guidelines/undergraduate-portfolios

Scholarships Offered
All applicants including international students are eligible for merit-scholarships. The May and Paul Poetter Scholarship awards full tuition and is based on academic achievement. The Frances Larkin McCommon Scholarship awards full tuition and is based on artistic achievement. SCAD also offers SCAD academic scholarships ($1,500-$12,000). Among grands, the SCAD Athletic Grant awards $2,000-$12,000. For more information, visit: https://www.scad.edu/admission/financial-aid-and-scholarships

Special Opportunities
The School of Entertainment Arts offers a BFA in Sound Design.

High school students may earn college credits through joint enrollment and SCAD's Rising Star program as well as participate in SCAD Summer Seminars. Production design students can study away in Orlando, FL, Lacoste, France, and Berlin, Germany.

ALABAMA

ARKANSAS

DELAWARE

DISTRICT OF COLUMBIA

FLORIDA

GEORGIA

KENTUCKY

LOUISIANA

MARYLAND

MISSISSIPPI

NORTH CAROLINA

OKLAHOMA

SOUTH CAROLINA

TENNESSEE

TEXAS

VIRGINIA

WEST VIRGINIA

SOUTH

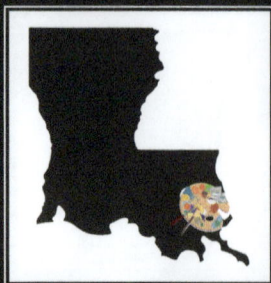

ALABAMA

ARKANSAS

DELAWARE

DISTRICT OF
COLUMBIA

FLORIDA

GEORGIA

KENTUCKY

LOUISIANA

MARYLAND

MISSISSIPPI

NORTH CAROLINA

OKLAHOMA

SOUTH CAROLINA

TENNESSEE

TEXAS

VIRGINIA

WEST VIRGINIA

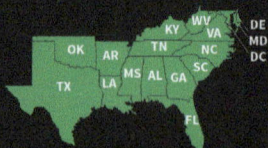

TULANE UNIVERSITY

Address: 6823 St. Charles Ave., New Orleans, LA 70118
Website: https://liberalarts.tulane.edu/departments/theatre-dance/programs/undergraduate/theatre
Contact: https://liberalarts.tulane.edu/departments/theatre-dance/contact-us
Request for Information: https://architecture.tulane.edu/prospective-students/mailing-list
Phone: (504) 865-5389
Email: undergrad.admission@tulane.edu

COST OF ATTENDANCE:

Tuition & Fees: $60,814 | **Additional Expenses:** $18,828
Total: $80,232

Financial Aid: https://admission.tulane.edu/tuition-aid

ADDITIONAL INFORMATION:

Available Degree(s)

- BFA Theatre: Design/Production Emphasis
- BA Theatre: Design/Technology Emphasis

Freshman Portfolio Requirement

There is no portfolio requirement for incoming freshmen.

Scholarships Offered

Tulane University offers two full-tuition merit scholarships: the Deans' Honor Scholarship and the Paul Tulane Award; 1 total-cost merit scholarship: the Stamps Scholarship. Merit-based scholarships for international students include the Global Scholarship and the Brandt Dixon Scholarship. For more information, visit: https://admission.tulane.edu/tuition-aid

Special Opportunities

Theatre students have access to three theatres, a costume shop, and a scene shop.

The School of Liberal Arts offers a Creative Industries Certificate and related summer courses such as Innovative Strategy in Creative Arts Industries, Leadership Strategies in Creative Industries, and Legal Strategies for Creatives. For more information, visit: https://liberalarts.tulane.edu/academics/undergraduate-studies/creative-industries-certificate

Notable Alumni

- Meryl Poster: Academy Award-winning and Emmy-nominated Producer (*Project Runway*)
- Al Shea: Theatre Critic and Actor
- Howard Scott Warshaw: Documentary Filmmaker and Video Game Designer

CATAWBA COLLEGE

Address: 2300 W Innes St, Salisbury, NC 28144
Website: https://catawba.edu/academics/programs/
undergraduate/theatre-arts/
Contact: https://catawba.edu/contact-catawba/
Request for Information: https://catawba.edu/contact-catawba/
Phone: (704) 637-4402
Email: admission@catawba.edu

COST OF ATTENDANCE:

Tuition & Fees: $32,380 | **Additional Expenses:** $15,964
Total: $48,344

Financial Aid: https://catawba.edu/about/offices/finaid/

ADDITIONAL INFORMATION:

Available Degree(s)

- BFA Theatre Arts, concentration: Design and Production

Freshman Portfolio Requirement

There is no portfolio requirement.

Scholarships Offered

Merit-based scholarships offered at Catawba College include two full-tuition scholarships: the Socratic Scholarship and the Spirit of Catawba Scholarship. For more information, visit: https://catawba.edu/about/offices/finaid/types-financial-aid/scholarships/merit-scholarships/

The Theatre Arts program awards an invitation-only full-tuition scholarship—the Burnet Hobgood Theatre Arts Scholarship. Qualified candidates must have a minimum unweighted GPA of 3.75. For more information, visit: https://catawba.edu/academics/programs/undergraduate/theatre-arts/student-resources/scholarships/scholarship/

Special Opportunities

Through a unique partnership with Lee Street theatre in Salisbury, Theatre Arts majors at Catawba College may take advantage of a semester-long production internship. Theatre Arts majors have studied abroad in England, Italy, Costa Rica, Greece, Germany, Japan, and Estonia.

The School of Performing Arts offers a BS in Theatre Arts Administration.

Notable Alumni

- Gerald "Jerry" Archer: Entertainment Technician at Walt Disney World
- Sean "Shaggy" Sears & Liam Macik: Founders of Throughline Theatre Company
- Brooke Beall: Scenic Artist at Alliance Theatre

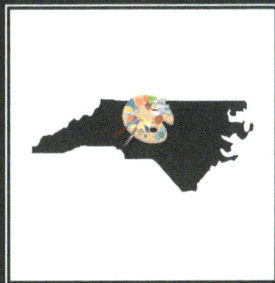

ALABAMA
ARKANSAS
DELAWARE
DISTRICT OF
COLUMBIA
FLORIDA
GEORGIA
KENTUCKY
LOUISIANA
MARYLAND
MISSISSIPPI
NORTH CAROLINA
OKLAHOMA
SOUTH CAROLINA
TENNESSEE
TEXAS
VIRGINIA
WEST VIRGINIA

SOUTH

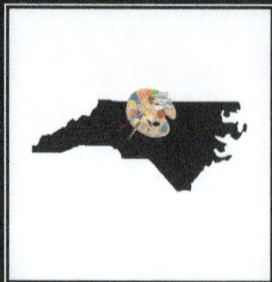

ALABAMA

ARKANSAS

DELAWARE

DISTRICT OF COLUMBIA

FLORIDA

GEORGIA

KENTUCKY

LOUISIANA

MARYLAND

MISSISSIPPI

NORTH CAROLINA

OKLAHOMA

SOUTH CAROLINA

TENNESSEE

TEXAS

VIRGINIA

WEST VIRGINIA

ELON UNIVERSITY

Address: 100 Campus Drive, Elon, NC 27244
Website: https://www.elon.edu/u/academics/arts-and-sciences/performing-arts/
Contact: https://www.elon.edu/u/about/contact-elon/
Request for Information: N/A
Phone: (336) 278-2000
Email: admissions@elon.edu

COST OF ATTENDANCE:

Tuition & Fees: $38,725 | **Additional Expenses:** $16,922
Total: $55,647

Financial Aid: https://www.elon.edu/u/admissions/undergraduate/financial-aid/

ADDITIONAL INFORMATION:

Available Degree(s)

- BA Theatrical Design & Technology

Freshman Portfolio Requirement

- Submit via Acceptd
- Personal Statement (video or written, 200-300 words)
- Resume
- Letters of Recommendation
- Samples of your work

For more information, visit: https://app.getacceptd.com/elon

Scholarships Offered

Elon University offers numerous merit-based scholarships, talent-based scholarships including Performing Arts Scholarships, as well as Fellows and Scholars programs (scholarships ranging from $7,500 to $13,500 per year). For more information, visit: https://www.elon.edu/u/admissions/undergraduate/financial-aid/scholarships/

Special Opportunities

Elon By Design, an "original design-thinking program," hosts workshops, events, and internship opportunities. For more information, visit: https://www.elon.edu/u/elon-by-design/

Design and Technology majors may study abroad in Italy, Spain, Greece, and at Theatre Academy London in England. There are also domestic study away opportunities in Chicago, Los Angeles, and New York City, where students can take courses such as LA Entertainment Production and participate in the Comedy Studies at Second City program. For more information, visit: https://elon.studioabroad.com/index.cfm?FuseAction=Programs.AdvancedSearch

The College of Arts and Sciences offers a BA in Arts Administration.

UNIVERSITY OF NORTH CAROLINA SCHOOL OF THE ARTS

Address: 1533 S Main St, Winston-Salem, NC 27127
Website: https://www.uncsa.edu/design-production/
undergraduate-programs/costume-design-technology.aspx
Contact: https://www.uncsa.edu/contact-uncsa.aspx
Request for Information: https://www.uncsa.edu/contact-uncsa.aspx
Phone: (336) 770-3399
Email: admissions@uncsa.edu

COST OF ATTENDANCE:

In-State Tuition & Fees: $9,338 | **Additional Expenses:** $12,987
Total: $22,325

Out-of-State Tuition & Fees: $25,081 | **Additional Expenses:** $12,987
Total: $36,568

Financial Aid: https://www.uncsa.edu/financialaid/index.aspx

ADDITIONAL INFORMATION:

Available Degree(s)
- BFA Costume Design & Technology
- BFA Lighting
- BFA Scene Design
- BFA Scene Painting
- BFA Scenic Technology
- BFA Sound Design
- BFA Stage Management
- BFA Stage Properties
- BFA Wig & Makeup Design

Freshman Portfolio Requirement
- All programs listed here require a portfolio
- All require materials related to the major and artistic work outside of theatre
- Some majors require a pre-screen, such as the BFA in Lighting and the BFA in Wig & Makeup Design

For detailed information on portfolio requirements, visit:
https://www.uncsa.edu/admissions/design-production/
undergraduate/portfolio-requirements.aspx

Scholarships Offered
University of North Carolina School of the Arts offers merit-based scholarships including the Kenan Excellence Scholarship, which provides full tuition, fees, and room and board for five students. For more information, visit: https://www.uncsa.edu/financialaid/types-of-aid.aspx

Special Opportunities
High school sophomores and juniors may apply to the one or two-year Visual Arts program at the School of Design & Production. Furthermore, UNCSA offers international trips for students to study abroad, most of which are by invitation only.

Notable Alumni
- Paul Tazewell: Emmy and Tony Award-Winning Costume Designer (*Hamilton, The Wiz Live!*, and *Jesus Christ Superstar Live In Concert*)
- Suri Bieler: Owner of Eclectic/Encore Props, "the largest prop rental house on the East Coast"
- Tanase Popa: Film and TV Producer, 5-time Emmy Award nominee

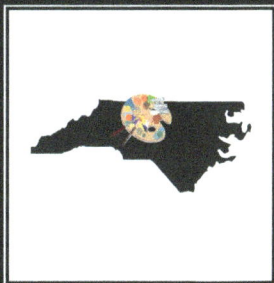

ALABAMA
ARKANSAS
DELAWARE
DISTRICT OF COLUMBIA
FLORIDA
GEORGIA
KENTUCKY
LOUISIANA
MARYLAND
MISSISSIPPI
NORTH CAROLINA
OKLAHOMA
SOUTH CAROLINA
TENNESSEE
TEXAS
VIRGINIA
WEST VIRGINIA

SOUTH

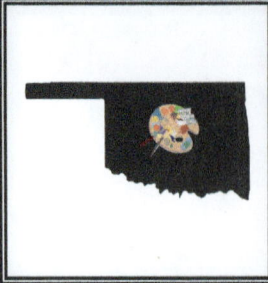

OKLAHOMA CITY UNIVERSITY

Address: 2501 N. Blackwelder, Oklahoma City, OK 73106
Website: https://www.okcu.edu/theatre/home/
Contact: https://www.okcu.edu/main/contact/
Request for Information: https://www.okcu.edu/admissions/requestinfo/
Phone: (405) 208-5000
Email: Contact via contact form or phone.

COST OF ATTENDANCE:

Tuition & Fees: $33,404 | **Additional Expenses:** $16,276
Total: $49,680

Financial Aid: https://www.okcu.edu/financialaid/home/

ADDITIONAL INFORMATION:

Available Degree(s)

- BFA Design & Production, emphases:
  - Costume Design & Technology
  - Stage & Production Management
  - Lighting Design
  - Scenic Design
  - Props Design and Fabrication
  - Sound Design

Freshman Portfolio Requirement

- Portfolio that demonstrates technical skills
- Interview and resume

For more information, visit: https://www.okcu.edu/theatre/admissions

Scholarships Offered

Students in the School of Theatre are eligible for academic scholarships based on high school GPA and standardized test scores (up to $7,800 a year). For more information, visit: https://www.okcu.edu/financialaid/types-of-assistance/scholarships?overview=true

Special Opportunities

The School of Theatre has an exchange program with Rose Bruford College in London, through which stage management students may study abroad in the spring semester of their junior year. Theatre students can also study fashion design in Santa Reparata International School of Art in Florence, Italy.

Notable Alumni

- Travis Baldwin: Assistant Lighting Designer at Arizona Opera Company
- Breanna Hughey: Senior Production Manager at Princess Cruise Lines
- Jeremy Allen Fisher: Production Manager at Tennessee Shakespeare Company

UNIVERSITY OF OKLAHOMA

Address: 660 Parrington Oval, Norman, OK 73019
Website: http://www.ou.edu/finearts/drama
Contact: http://www.ou.edu/web/about_ou/contact
Request for Information: Press "Request More Information" -
http://www.ou.edu/admissions
Phone: (405) 325-0311
Email: admissions@ou.edu

COST OF ATTENDANCE:

In-State Tuition & Fees: $13,065 | **Additional Expenses:** $11,700
Total: $24,765

Out-of-State Tuition & Fees: $28,869 | **Additional Expenses:** $18,757
Total: $40,569

Financial Aid: http://www.ou.edu/admissions/affordability/
financial-aid

ADDITIONAL INFORMATION:

Available Degree(s)
- BFA Drama, emphasis: Design, tracks:
  - o Scenic Design
  - o Costume Design
  - o Lighting Design
  - o Sound Design
- BFA Theatre, emphasis: Stage Management

Freshman Portfolio Requirement
All programs listed here require the following:

- Headshot, resume, and statement
- Letters of recommendation
- Interview, either virtually or in person
- Drawings and artwork
- Theatrical design work and photographs of completed projects
- Other materials related to the major of choice

For more information, visit: https://app.getacceptd.com/oklahoma

Scholarships Offered
University of Oklahoma offers numerous test score and high school
GPA-based scholarships (up to $16,000 over four years for in-state
students and $60,000 over four years for out-of-state students and
and international students) as well as National Merit Scholarships,
Oklahoma State Regents' Academic Scholars Program scholarship
and test-optional scholarships. For more information, visit: https://
www.ou.edu/admissions/affordability/scholarships

The School of Drama also awards scholarships ranging from $500 to
$6,000 after on-campus interview upon acceptance into the program.

Special Opportunities
Students have access to five theatres, including the Holmberg Hall,
a European-style performance hall, costume and scene shops, a
variety of lighting consoles, and sound equipment.

Notable Alumni
- Adam Honoré: Broadway and Off-Broadway Lighting Designer
  (*Chicken and Biscuits, Fun Home*)
- Carol Sue Littleton: winner of Emmy Award for Outstanding
  Single Camera Picture Editing for a
  Miniseries, Movie or a Special (*Tuesdays
  with Morrie*)
- Sterlin Harjo: Filmmaker

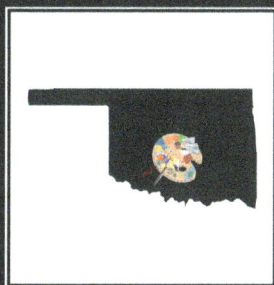

ALABAMA

ARKANSAS

DELAWARE

DISTRICT OF
COLUMBIA

FLORIDA

GEORGIA

KENTUCKY

LOUISIANA

MARYLAND

MISSISSIPPI

NORTH CAROLINA

OKLAHOMA

SOUTH CAROLINA

TENNESSEE

TEXAS

VIRGINIA

WEST VIRGINIA

SOUTH

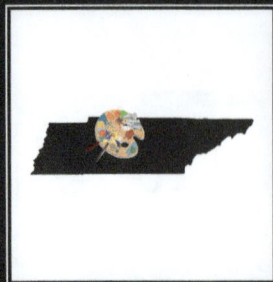

ALABAMA

ARKANSAS

DELAWARE

DISTRICT OF
COLUMBIA

FLORIDA

GEORGIA

KENTUCKY

LOUISIANA

MARYLAND

MISSISSIPPI

NORTH CAROLINA

OKLAHOMA

SOUTH CAROLINA

TENNESSEE

TEXAS

VIRGINIA

WEST VIRGINIA

BELMONT UNIVERSITY

Address: 1900 Belmont Blvd, Nashville, TN 37212
Website: https://www.belmont.edu/cmpa/theatre-dance/
undergrad/index.html
Contact: https://www.belmont.edu/admissions/index.html
Request for Information: https://campsite.bio/belmontadmissions
Phone: (615) 460-6000
Email: N/A

COST OF ATTENDANCE:

Tuition & Fees: $38,430 | **Additional Expenses:** $19,875
Total: $58,305

Financial Aid: https://www.belmont.edu/sfs/aid/undergrad.html

ADDITIONAL INFORMATION:

Available Degree(s)

- BFA Theatre, concentration: Production Design

Freshman Portfolio Requirement

- Emphasis in design and technical experience
- Any combination of drawings, renderings, draftings, CAD
  drawings, light plots, etc.
- Theatre resume
- Headshot

For more information, visit: https://www.belmont.edu/cmpa/
theatre-dance/apply.html

Scholarships Offered

All applicants are automatically considered for merit scholarships
offered at Belmont University. Students who apply test-optional
will be considered for merit scholarships based on their high school
GPA and overall strength of their application. General Freshman
Academic Merit Scholarships ($3,000 to $10,000 annually) are
awarded on a rolling basis following the offer of admission. Belmont
also offers named awards, which recognize approximately the top
two percent of all freshman applicants. Other scholarships include
the Leadership Scholarships ($3,000). For more information, visit:
https://www.belmont.edu/sfs/scholarships/merit.html

Special Opportunities

The Department of Theatre and Dance offers semester-long sessions
and Maymester sessions in locations such as London, Berlin,
Athens, and Prague. Students can also spend a semester studying
away in New York City and Los Angeles.

BAYLOR UNIVERSITY

Address: 1311 S 5th St, Waco, TX 76706
Website: https://www.baylor.edu/theatre/index.php?id=947435
Contact: https://www.baylor.edu/admissions/index.php?id=871966
Request for Information: N/A
Phone: (254) 710-3436
Email: admissions@baylor.edu

COST OF ATTENDANCE:

Tuition & Fees: $50,232 | **Additional Expenses:** $12,682
Total: $62,914

Financial Aid: https://www.baylor.edu/admissions/index.php?id=871964

ADDITIONAL INFORMATION:

Available Degree(s)

- BFA Theatre Design and Technology, specializations:
  - Costume and Makeup Design
  - Lighting Design
  - Scenic Design & Technology
  - Sound & Media Design
  - Stage Management

Freshman Portfolio Requirement

- Interview required, virtually
- Portfolio including past work in theatre and art in general
- Portfolio may be a digital notebook, collection of pictures, website, etc.

For more information, visit: https://www.baylor.edu/theatre/index.php?id=947469

Scholarships Offered

All applicants to Baylor University, including students who apply as test optional and first-time international students, are automatically considered for academic scholarships. Other awards include a scholarship valued at approximately $60,000 per year at the Getterman Scholars Program and a full-tuition awards at the Invitation to Excellence program. For more information, visit: https://www.baylor.edu/admissions/index.php?id=873057&WT.ac=AcademicScholarshipsPS

Special Opportunities

The theatre department gathers weekly to observe student-produced work and other presentations, which prospective students are encouraged to attend.

Every two years, students may participate in a European study abroad program, which has included lengthy stays in England or France. This program has also brought students to Italy, Greece, Belgium, and Ireland.

The theatre department co-sponsors the Fine Arts Living Learning Center, a community of student artists just next door to Baylor's premiere Fine Arts facilities.

ALABAMA
ARKANSAS
DELAWARE
DISTRICT OF COLUMBIA
FLORIDA
GEORGIA
KENTUCKY
LOUISIANA
MARYLAND
MISSISSIPPI
NORTH CAROLINA
OKLAHOMA
SOUTH CAROLINA
TENNESSEE
TEXAS
VIRGINIA
WEST VIRGINIA

SOUTH

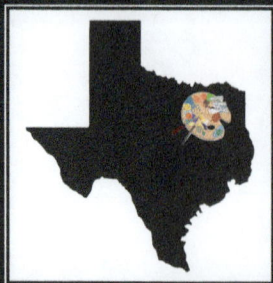

ALABAMA

ARKANSAS

DELAWARE

DISTRICT OF
COLUMBIA

FLORIDA

GEORGIA

KENTUCKY

LOUISIANA

MARYLAND

MISSISSIPPI

NORTH CAROLINA

OKLAHOMA

SOUTH CAROLINA

TENNESSEE

TEXAS

VIRGINIA

WEST VIRGINIA

TEXAS CHRISTIAN UNIVERSITY (TCU)

Address: 2800 South University Dr., Fort Worth, TX 76109
Website: https://finearts.tcu.edu/theatre/academics/areas-of-study/bfa-emphasis-in-design/
Contact: https://admissions.tcu.edu/connect.php
Request for Information: https://www.tcu.edu/inquire.php
Phone: (817) 257-7000
Email: frogmail@tcu.edu

COST OF ATTENDANCE:

Tuition & Fees: $51,660 | **Additional Expenses:** $20,168
Total: $71,828

Financial Aid: https://financialaid.tcu.edu/

ADDITIONAL INFORMATION:

Available Degree(s)

- BFA Theatre, emphasis: Design & Technology

Freshman Portfolio Requirement

- Interview required, virtually or in-person
- Prescreen must be passed for interview to be offered
- Portfolio with drawings, paintings, theatre designs, stage manager book samples, pictures of created props or scenery, etc.
- Wildcard (optional): Interesting story about yourself, passionate speech, etc. (60 seconds maximum)
- 2 letters of reference
- Theatrical/artistic resume
- Photograph
- 1-page personal statement

For more information, visit: https://finearts.tcu.edu/theatre/admission/auditions-and-portfolio-review/

Scholarships Offered

Academic scholarships for first-year students are awarded based primarily on a combination of grades, ACT or SAT score, and curriculum rigor. All students admitted to the BFA Theatre program will receive a scholarship of at least $2,000 per year. For more information, visit: https://admissions.tcu.edu/afford/scholarship-aid/index.php

The Department of Theatre awards the Nordan Fine Arts Scholarships (approximately $15,000 per year) and 35-40 production grants ($3,000 - $6,000 per year) in return for 10 hours per week of theatre production work. For more information, visit: https://finearts.tcu.edu/theatre/admission/scholarships/

Special Opportunities

The average class size for BFA design and technology is 12 students. All BFA Theatre majors serve on a production crew each semester, rotating between various roles.

SHENANDOAH UNIVERSITY

Address: 1460 University Dr, Winchester, VA 22601
Website: https://www.su.edu/conservatory/areas-of-study/
theatre-design-and-production/
Contact: https://www.su.edu/admissions/contact-us/
Request for Information: https://www.su.edu/conservatory/
areas-of-study/acting/
Phone: (540) 665-4581
Email: Admit@su.edu

COST OF ATTENDANCE:

Tuition & Fees: $33,140 | **Additional Expenses:** $16,442
Total: $49,582

Financial Aid: https://www.su.edu/financial-aid/

ADDITIONAL INFORMATION:

Available Degree(s)
- BFA Theatre Design & Production, emphases:
  - Costume Design
  - Lighting Design
  - Scenic Design
  - Sound Design and Reinforcement
  - Stage Management
  - Technical Production

Freshman Portfolio Requirement
- Interview on audition day
- Resume
- Costume Design, Lighting Design, Scenic Design, and
  Technical Production:
  - Photographs, draftings, design sketches, and letters of
    recommendation that relate to the area of emphasis
- Sound Design and Reinforcement
  - Include works related to this area of emphasis along
    with letters of recommendation
- Stage Management
  - Include prompt book or best production materials along
    with letters of recommendation

For more information, visit: https://www.su.edu/admissions/
future-freshmen/application-information/conservatory-audition-
requirements/audition-faqs/

Scholarships Offered
Theatre students may be eligible for the Shenandoah University
Conservatory Scholarship, valued at $2000-$19,500 per year. This
renewable scholarship is based on the student's application and
the audition. All students may be eligible for other merit-based
awards, ranging in value from $3,000-$20,000 per year. For more
information, visit: https://www.su.edu/financial-aid/incoming-
undergraduates/scholarships/

Special Opportunities
The Shenandoah Conservatory offers an online Performing Arts
Leadership and Management (4+1) Accelerated Program.

Notable Alumni
- Emily Vandervort Heilig: Lecturer, Costume Technology
  and Costume Crafts Supervisor at The University of North
  Carolina, Greensboro
- Elspeth Ridout McCormick: Artistic
  Concepts Group in Virginia
- Madeline Woods: Tessitura Database
  Coordinator at Baltimore Center Stage

ALABAMA

ARKANSAS

DELAWARE

DISTRICT OF
COLUMBIA

FLORIDA

GEORGIA

KENTUCKY

LOUISIANA

MARYLAND

MISSISSIPPI

NORTH CAROLINA

OKLAHOMA

SOUTH CAROLINA

TENNESSEE

TEXAS

VIRGINIA

WEST VIRGINIA

SOUTH

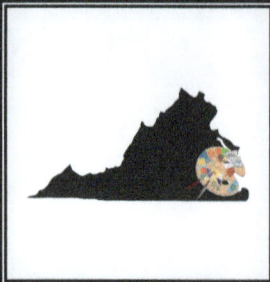

ALABAMA

ARKANSAS

DELAWARE

DISTRICT OF
COLUMBIA

FLORIDA

GEORGIA

KENTUCKY

LOUISIANA

MARYLAND

MISSISSIPPI

NORTH CAROLINA

OKLAHOMA

SOUTH CAROLINA

TENNESSEE

TEXAS

VIRGINIA

WEST VIRGINIA

VIRGINIA COMMONWEALTH UNIVERSITY

Address: Virginia Commonwealth University, Richmond, VA 23284
Website: https://arts.vcu.edu/academics/departments/theatre/
Contact: https://www.vcu.edu/contacts/
Request for Information: https://www.vcu.edu/admissions/
contact-admissions/ugrad-interest-form/
Phone: (804) 828-0100
Email: ugrad@vcu.edu

COST OF ATTENDANCE:

In-State Tuition & Fees: $17,140 | **Additional Expenses:** $17,549
Total: $34,689

Out-of-State Tuition & Fees: $38,478 | **Additional Expenses:** $17,549
Total: $56,027

Financial Aid: https://finaid.vcu.edu/

ADDITIONAL INFORMATION:

Available Degree(s)

- BFA Theatre, concentrations:
  o Costume Design
  o Lighting Design
  o Scenic Design
  o Stage Management

Freshman Portfolio Requirement

- Submit via SlideRoom
- Theatrical resume
- Portfolio of 12-16 images, with a diverse range of 2D and 3D media
- Callback or interview required where students must present their portfolio

For more information, visit: https://arts.vcu.edu/admissions/how-to-apply/freshman-applicants/freshman-applicants-theatre/

Scholarships Offered

First-year students are automatically considered for VCUarts talent scholarships ($5,000-$12,000 annually) based on academic merit and artistic talent. University awards vary based on the scholarship, but range from $8,000 per year to $16,000 plus room and board per year. For more information, visit: https://arts.vcu.edu/admissions/scholarships/

Special Opportunities

VCUarts Qatar is the sister campus located in Doha, Qatar. Design students may apply to spend a semester at this campus. Additionally, students may study abroad through faculty-led programs in Korea and Italy as well as VCU-affiliated programs. For more information, visit: https://arts.vcu.edu/academics/travel-study-abroad/

CHAPTER 16

CHAPTER 16

REGION FOUR

WEST

ALASKA

ARIZONA

CALIFORNIA

COLORADO

HAWAII

IDAHO

MONTANA

NEVADA

NEW MEXICO

OREGON

UTAH

WASHINGTON

WYOMING

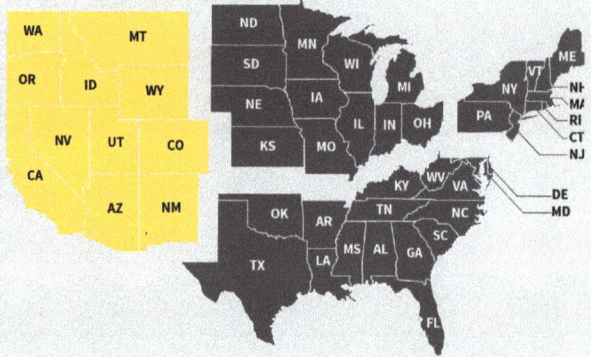

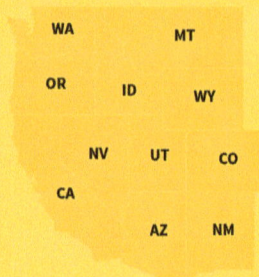

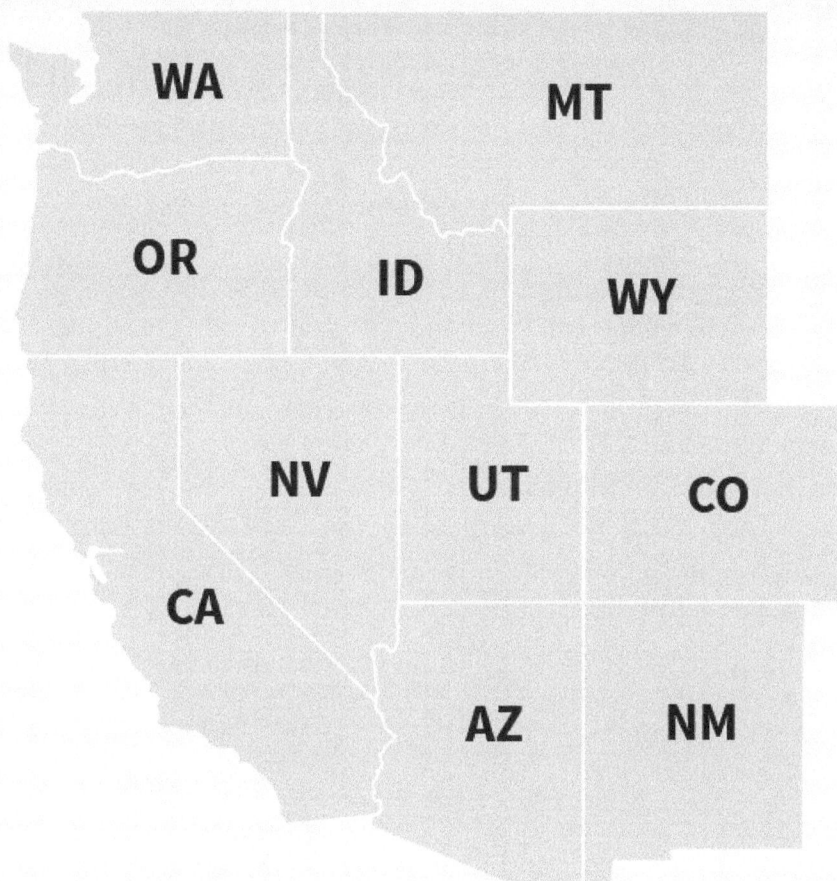

1. *AZ – University of Arizona*
2. *CA – Academy of Art University*
3. *CA – California Institute of the Arts (CalArts)*
4. *CA – Loyola Marymount University (LMU)*
5. *CA – Otis College of Art and Design*
6. *CA – Pepperdine University*
7. *CA – University of California, Los Angeles (UCLA)*
8. *CA – University of Southern California (USC)*
9. *NV – University of Nevada, Las Vegas (UNLV)*
10. *WA – Cornish College of the Arts*
11. *WA – Gonzaga University*

COSTUME DESIGN & TECHNICAL THEATRE SCHOOLS

School	Avg. GPA, SAT Evidence-Based Reading Writing (ERW), SAT Math (M), and ACT Composite (C) Early Decision (ED): Yes/No	Admission Statistics	Program(s)	Portfolio, Interview, and/or Audition Required (Req.)
University of Arizona The University of Arizona, Tucson, AZ 85721	GPA: 3.43 SAT (ERW): 550-660 SAT (M): 540-690 ACT (C): 21-29 ED: No	Admit Rate: 85% Undergrad Enrollment: 35,357 Total Enrollment: 45,601	BFA Theatre Production – Design & Technical Production, specializations: Costume Design Costume Production Lighting Design and Production Stage Management Sound Design Scenic Design Technical Direction Degrees Awarded in the Program(s) (2020): 27	Portfolio: Req. Interview: Not req. Audition: Not req.
Academy of Art University 79 New Montgomery St., San Francisco, CA 94105	GPA: N/A SAT (ERW): N/A SAT (M): N/A ACT (C): N/A *Academy of Art has an open admission policy. ED: No	Admit Rate: N/A Undergrad Enrollment: 6,124 Total Enrollment: 8,928	BFA Costume Design	Portfolio: Not req. Interview: Not req. Audition: Not req.

School	Avg. GPA, SAT Evidence-Based Reading Writing (ERW), SAT Math (M), and ACT Composite (C) Early Decision (ED): Yes/No	Admission Statistics	Program(s)	Portfolio, Interview, and/or Audition Required (Req.)
California Institute of the Arts (CalArts) 24700 McBean Pkwy., Valencia, CA 91355	GPA: N/A SAT (ERW): N/A SAT (M): N/A ACT (C): N/A *CalArts is test optional. ED: No	Admit Rate: 27% Undergrad Enrollment: 762 Total Enrollment: 1,166 Program Completion (2020): 18	BFA Experience Design and Production, specializations: Costume Design Experience Design/Themed Entertainment Lighting Design Scene Design Sound Design Stage Management Technical Direction Degrees Awarded in the Program(s) (2020): 18	Portfolio: Req. Interview: Req. Audition: Not req.
Loyola Marymount University (LMU) 1 LMU Dr., Los Angeles, CA 90045	GPA: 3.85 SAT (ERW): 610-690 SAT (M): 600-700 ACT (C): 27-31 ED: Yes	Admit Rate: 50% Undergrad Enrollment: 6,673 Total Enrollment: 9,686	BA Theatre, emphasis: Design Degrees Awarded in the Program(s) (2020): N/A	Portfolio: Optional, recommended Interview: Not req. Audition: Not req.

WEST

COSTUME DESIGN & TECHNICAL THEATRE SCHOOLS

School	Avg. GPA, SAT Evidence-Based Reading Writing (ERW), SAT Math (M), and ACT Composite (C) Early Decision (ED): Yes/No	Admission Statistics	Program(s)	Portfolio, Interview, and/or Audition Required (Req.)
Otis College of Art and Design 9045 Lincoln Blvd., Los Angeles, CA 90045	GPA: 3.26 SAT (ERW): N/A SAT (M): N/A ACT (C): N/A *Otis College of Art and Design is test optional. ED: No	Admit Rate: 80% Undergrad Enrollment: 1,030 Total Enrollment: 1,073	BFA Fashion Design, emphasis: Costume Design Degrees Awarded in the Program(s) (2020): 21	Portfolio: Req. Interview: Not req. Audition: Not req.
Pepperdine University 24255 Pacific Coast Hwy, Malibu, CA 90263	GPA: 3.69 SAT (ERW): 600-690 SAT (M): 600-720 ACT (C): 26-31 ED: No	Admit Rate: 42% Undergrad Enrollment: 3,459 Total Enrollment: 9,554	BA Theatre Arts, emphasis: Production Design Degrees Awarded in the Program(s) (2020): 9	Portfolio: Req. Interview: Req. Audition: Not req.
University of California, Los Angeles (UCLA) 405 Hilgard Avenue, Los Angeles, CA 90095	GPA: 3.9 SAT (ERW): 640-740 SAT (M): 640-790 ACT (C): 27-34 ED: No	Admit Rate: 14% Undergrad Enrollment: 31,636 Total Enrollment: 44,589	BA Theater, emphasis: Design/Production Degrees Awarded in the Program(s) (2020): N/A	Portfolio: Req. Interview: UCLA may require it to gain more information about applicant. Audition: Not req.

School	Avg. GPA, SAT Evidence-Based Reading Writing (ERW), SAT Math (M), and ACT Composite (C) Early Decision (ED): Yes/No	Admission Statistics	Program(s)	Portfolio, Interview, and/or Audition Required (Req.)
University of Southern California (USC) 1029 Childs Way, Los Angeles, CA 90089	GPA: 3.83 SAT (ERW): 660-740 SAT (M): 680-790 ACT (C): 30-34 ED: No	Admit Rate: 16% Undergrad Enrollment: 19,786 Total Enrollment: 46,287	BFA Design BFA Sound Design BFA Stage Management BFA Technical Direction Degrees Awarded in the Program(s) (2020): 7	Portfolio: Req. Interview: Req. Audition: Not req.
University of Nevada, Las Vegas (UNLV) 4505 S Maryland Pkwy, Las Vegas, NV 89154	GPA: 3.43 SAT (ERW): 520-620 SAT (M): 510-630 ACT (C): 19-25 ED: No	Admit Rate: 81% Undergrad Enrollment: 25,864 Total Enrollment: 31,142	BA Theatre, concentration: Design/Technology Degrees Awarded in the Program(s) (2020): 16	Portfolio: Not req. Interview: Not req. Audition: Not req.

WEST

COSTUME DESIGN & TECHNICAL THEATRE SCHOOLS

School	Avg. GPA, SAT Evidence-Based Reading Writing (ERW), SAT Math (M), and ACT Composite (C) Early Decision (ED): Yes/No	Admission Statistics	Program(s)	Portfolio, Interview, and/ or Audition Required (Req.)
Cornish College of the Arts 1000 Lenora St, Seattle, WA 98121	GPA: N/A SAT (ERW): N/A SAT (M): N/A ACT (C): N/A *Cornish College of the Arts is test optional. ED: No	Admit Rate: 79% Undergrad Enrollment: 482 Total Enrollment: 482	BFA Performance Production, concentrations: Costume Design Lighting Design Scenic Design Sound Design Stage Management Degrees Awarded in the Program(s) (2020): 9	Portfolio: Interview: Audition:
Gonzaga University 502 E Boone Ave, Spokane, WA 99258	GPA: 3.69 SAT (ERW): 580-670 SAT (M): 580-680 ACT (C): 25-30 ED: No	Admit Rate: 73% Undergrad Enrollment: 4,852 Total Enrollment: 7,295	BA Theatre Arts, concentration: Design, Technology, & Management Degrees Awarded in the Program(s) (2020): 2	Portfolio: Not req. Interview: Optional Audition: Not req.

ALASKA

ARIZONA

CALIFORNIA

COLORADO

HAWAII

IDAHO

MONTANA

NEVADA

NEW MEXICO

OREGON

UTAH

WASHINGTON

WYOMING

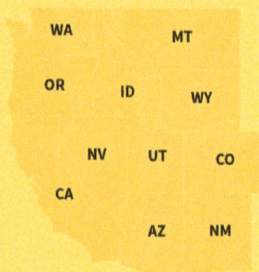

UNIVERSITY OF ARIZONA

Address: The University of Arizona, Tucson, AZ 85721
Website: https://tftv.arizona.edu/prospective-students/design-technical-production/
Contact: https://www.arizona.edu/contact-us
Request for Information: https://admissions.arizona.edu/request-info
Phone: (520) 621-2211
Email: admissions@arizona.edu

COST OF ATTENDANCE:

In-State Tuition & Fees: $12,700 | **Additional Expenses:** $18,050
Total: $30,750

Out-of-State Tuition & Fees: $37,200 | **Additional Expenses:** $18,050
Total: $55,250

Financial Aid: https://financialaid.arizona.edu/

ADDITIONAL INFORMATION:

Available Degree(s)
- BFA Theatre Production – Design & Technical Production, specializations:
  - Costume Design
  - Costume Production
  - Lighting Design and Production
  - Stage Management
  - Sound Design
  - Scenic Design
  - Technical Direction

Freshman Portfolio Requirement
- Portfolio with no more than 10 examples of artwork or technical skills
- Resume
- Reference
- Essay

For more information, visit: https://tftv.arizona.edu/admissions/admissions-prospective-students/

Scholarships Offered
The School of Theatre, Film & Television offers Theatre Student Awards such as the Baker Theatrical Lighting Scholarship and the G. Ann Blackmarr Endowment. For more information, visit: https://tftv.arizona.edu/facilities-resources/scholarships/

Special Opportunities
Theatre students have access to three theatres, a scenery shop, a costume shop, and a warehouse of stock. Students can also take advantage of two levels of stage combat class.

Notable Alumni
- Philip Rosenberg: Broadway and Off-Broadway Lighting Designer (*Mrs. Doubtfire* the Musical, *Pretty Woman* the Musical, and *A Gentleman's Guide to Love and Murder*)
- Elaine "E.E." Moe: Artistic Director and Co-Founder of Megaw Theatre and Actors Studio
- Shannon Kolder: Founder of Kolder Productions

ACADEMY OF ART UNIVERSITY

Address: 79 New Montgomery St., San Francisco, CA 94105
Website: https://www.academyart.edu/academics/fashion/
Contact: https://my.academyart.edu/directories/admissions
Request for Information: https://www.academyart.edu/form-request-information/
Phone: (800) 544-2787
Email: admissions@academyart.edu

COST OF ATTENDANCE:

Tuition & Fees: $26,399 | **Additional Expenses:** N/A
Total: $26,399

Financial Aid: https://www.academyart.edu/finances/types-of-financial-aid/

ADDITIONAL INFORMATION:

Available Degree(s)

- BFA Costume Design

Freshman Portfolio Requirement

There is no portfolio. This is an open-admissions school.

Scholarships Offered

The Emerging Artist Scholarship offers awards up to $3,000. International Art & Design Scholarship awards a limited number of scholarships (up to $2,000) to international students. For more information, visit: https://www.academyart.edu/finances/scholarships/

Special Opportunities

The Academy houses a 3D Pattern Making Lab, a knitting studio, a pattern making studio, a styling closet, and a textile lab. The textile lab is fully equipped with 700 silkscreens, repeat yardage tables, UV exposure units, and pigments and dyes.

Every year, the School of Fashion awards two full-tuition scholarships for students who have passed the DELF B1 to study in Paris with Studio Berçot. Two students are selected to spend a year or a semester at the Fashion Department of Kingston University in London.

Notable Alumni

- Rick Baker: winner of Academy Award for Best Makeup and Hairstyling (*An American Werewolf in London*)

ALASKA

ARIZONA

CALIFORNIA

COLORADO

HAWAII

IDAHO

MONTANA

NEVADA

NEW MEXICO

OREGON

UTAH

WASHINGTON

WYOMING

WEST

ALASKA

ARIZONA

CALIFORNIA

COLORADO

HAWAII

IDAHO

MONTANA

NEVADA

NEW MEXICO

OREGON

UTAH

WASHINGTON

WYOMING

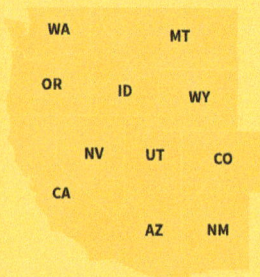

CALIFORNIA INSTITUTE OF THE ARTS

Address: 24700 McBean Pkwy., Valencia, CA 91355
Website: https://theater.calarts.edu/
Contact: https://calarts.edu/about/contact
Request for Information: https://calarts.edu/admissions/request-info
Phone: (661) 255-1050
Email: admissions@calarts.edu

COST OF ATTENDANCE:

Tuition & Fees: $47,446 | **Additional Expenses:** $19,705
Total: $67,151

Financial Aid: https://calarts.edu/tuition-and-financial-aid/financial-aid/overview

ADDITIONAL INFORMATION:

Available Degree(s)
- BFA Experience Design and Production, specializations:
  - Costume Design
  - Experience Design/Themed Entertainment
  - Lighting Design
  - Scene Design
  - Sound Design
  - Stage Management
  - Technical Direction

What is required for freshman portfolios or auditions?
The BFA in Experience Design and Production requires the following:

- Interview required
- Examples of drawings, paintings, drafting skills, and theatre design work
- Digital media and accompanying paperwork
- Scores optional
- Created installations
- Video introduction (30-90 seconds) following prompt

For more information on BFA Experience Design and Production requirements, visit: https://calarts.edu/admissions/portfolio-audition-requirements/theater/experience-design-and-production

Scholarships Offered
CalArts offers institutional scholarships that are awarded to students based on need and merit. All awards cover tuition only. In addition, they offer endowed and annually funded scholarships. For more information, visit: https://calarts.edu/tuition-and-financial-aid/financial-aid/types-of-financial-aid-2

Special Opportunities
The School of Theater hosts a scene shop, a scenic art studio, a costume shop, a light lab, a sound lab, and a media lab. Furthermore, pre-college students ages 14+ may take Portfolio Development Workshop at CalArts. For more information, visit: https://extendedstudies.calarts.edu/pre-college

Notable Alumni
- Leon Rothenberg: winner of Tony Award for Best Sound Design (*The Nance*)
- Kevin Adams: winner of Tony Award for Best Lighting Design of a Musical and Tony Award for Best Lighting Design of a Play (*Hedwig and the Angry Inch*)
- Jenny Foldenauer: winner of 2014 LA Stage Alliance Ovation award for Best Costume Design

LOYOLA MARYMOUNT UNIVERSITY (LMU)

Address: 1 LMU Dr., Los Angeles, CA 90045
Website: https://cfa.lmu.edu/programs/theatrearts/
Contact: https://cfa.lmu.edu/programs/theatrearts/contactus/
Request for Information: https://www.lmu.edu/about/contact/
Phone: (310) 338-2700
Email: admission@lmu.edu

COST OF ATTENDANCE:

Tuition & Fees: $53,067 | **Additional Expenses:** $14,551
Total: $67,618

Financial Aid: https://financialaid.lmu.edu/

ADDITIONAL INFORMATION:

Available Degree(s)

- BA Theatre, emphasis: Design

Freshman Portfolio Requirement

- Portfolio is optional. However it is recommended
- Strong letter of recommendation from high school drama teacher or supervisor

For more information, visit: https://cfa.lmu.edu/programs/theatrearts/admissions/auditionportfolio/

Scholarships Offered

The Trustee Scholarship awards full tuition, room, and board for four years and requires an on-campus interview. The Presidential Scholarship is also a merit-based opportunity that gifts $25,000 annually for four years. The Arrupe Scholarship (from $12,500 to full tuition) is available to domestic and international students and is renewable for four years. For more information, visit: https://financialaid.lmu.edu/prospectivestudents/scholarships/

Special Opportunities

Theatre majors are encouraged to study abroad at the Moscow Art Theater (MXAT). This program is a four-month conservatory-style program where students train with European theatre experts and LMU faculty. For more information, visit: https://cfa.lmu.edu/programs/theatrearts/academics/studyabroad/

Notable Alumni

- Amber White: Broadway Stage Manager (*Hamilton: An American Musical*)

ALASKA

ARIZONA

CALIFORNIA

COLORADO

HAWAII

IDAHO

MONTANA

NEVADA

NEW MEXICO

OREGON

UTAH

WASHINGTON

WYOMING

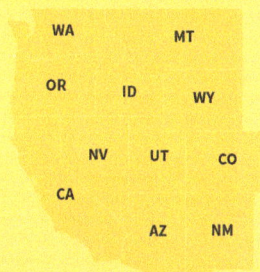

WEST

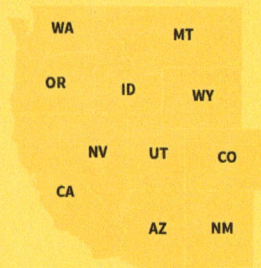

OTIS COLLEGE OF ART AND DESIGN

Address: 9045 Lincoln Blvd., Los Angeles, CA 90045
Website: https://cfa.lmu.edu/programs/theatrearts/
Contact: https://www.otis.edu/contact-otis-college-art-design
Request for Information: https://www.otis.edu/inquiry-form
Phone: (310) 665-6800
Email: admissions@otis.edu

COST OF ATTENDANCE:

Tuition & Fees: $47,700 | **Additional Expenses:** $21,354
Total: $69,054

Financial Aid: https://www.otis.edu/financial-aid

ADDITIONAL INFORMATION:

Available Degree(s)

- BFA Fashion Design, emphasis: Costume Design

Freshman Portfolio Requirement

- Submit via SlideRoom
- Option 1: Open Portfolio
  - o   10-20 examples of best and most recent work, direct observation works are encouraged
  - o   Artwork can be in any medium
- Option 2: Structured Portfolio (This option follows prompts)
  - o   3 images: Without showing person's face, create 3 images that are "portraits"
  - o   4 images: Tell a story related to a moment in your life
  - o   3 images: Showcase places that are important to you
  - o   Additional works welcome outside of these 10

For more information, visit: https://www.otis.edu/portfolio

Scholarships Offered

Otis College Scholarships are awarded to students based on need, academic merit, and artistic merit. Otis Named Scholarships are awarded by donors such as Nike or Sony for students who maintain a 3.0+ GPA and typically require a recommendation from the department chair. Otis College also recommends students apply for outside scholarships. For more information, visit: https://www.otis.edu/financial-aid/scholarships

Special Opportunities

Through the AICAD Exchange program, students can spend a semester at a member school of the Association of Independent Colleges of Art & Design at no additional cost or loss of credit. For more information, visit: https://www.otis.edu/travel-study-programs/exchange-programs

Notable Alumni

- Dorothy Jeakins: winner of Academy Award for Best Costume Design (*Joan of Arc, The Night of the Iguana*)

ALASKA

ARIZONA

CALIFORNIA

COLORADO

HAWAII

IDAHO

MONTANA

NEVADA

NEW MEXICO

OREGON

UTAH

WASHINGTON

WYOMING

PEPPERDINE UNIVERSITY

Address: 24255 Pacific Coast Hwy, Malibu, CA 90263
Website: https://seaver.pepperdine.edu/fine-arts/undergraduate/theatre/
Contact: https://www.pepperdine.edu/contact/
Request for Information: https://seaver.pepperdine.edu/undergraduate/theatre/
Phone: (310) 506-4000
Email: admission-seaver@pepperdine.edu

COST OF ATTENDANCE:

Tuition & Fees: $59,450 | **Additional Expenses:** $20,770
Total: $80,220

Financial Aid: https://seaver.pepperdine.edu/admission/financial-aid/undergraduate/

ADDITIONAL INFORMATION:

Available Degree(s)

- BA Theatre Arts, emphasis: Production Design

Freshman Portfolio Requirement

- Interview required, virtually or in person
- Preferable to present portfolio in person with hard copies or with a digital device
- Upload via SlideRoom

For more information, visit: https://seaver.pepperdine.edu/fine-arts/audition/theatre/production-design.htm

Scholarships Offered

Pepperdine offers merit-based scholarships such as the Regents Scholarship and the George Pepperdine Achievement Award. For more information, visit: https://seaver.pepperdine.edu/admission/financial-aid/undergraduate/types/university-private.htm

The theatre program awards a Special Achievement Scholarship as well as the Ubben Endowed Scholarship for Production Design Majors ($25,000 per year).

Special Opportunities

Theatre Program offers the 8-week Edinburgh Summer Program in the summer.

Notable Alumni

- Michael W. Brown: Broadway Lighting Designer and Production Electrician (*Burn the Floor, Kinky Boots,* and *Let It Be*)
- Diggle: Broadway Scenic Designer (*Grand Horizons* and *Slave Play*)

ALASKA

ARIZONA

CALIFORNIA

COLORADO

HAWAII

IDAHO

MONTANA

NEVADA

NEW MEXICO

OREGON

UTAH

WASHINGTON

WYOMING

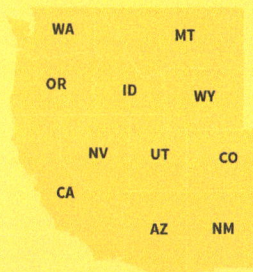

WEST

ALASKA

ARIZONA

CALIFORNIA

COLORADO

HAWAII

IDAHO

MONTANA

NEVADA

NEW MEXICO

OREGON

UTAH

WASHINGTON

WYOMING

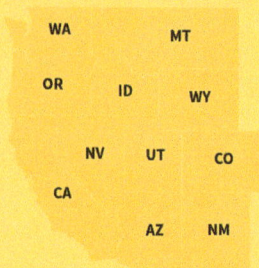

UNIVERSITY OF CALIFORNIA, LOS ANGELES

Address: 405 Hilgard Avenue, Los Angeles, CA 90095
Website: http://www.tft.ucla.edu/programs/theater-department/
Contact: http://www.tft.ucla.edu/contact/
Request for Information: https://connect.admission.ucla.edu/register/getconnected
Phone: (310) 206-8441
Email: info@tft.ucla.edu

COST OF ATTENDANCE:

In-State Tuition & Fees: $13,258 | **Additional Expenses:** $23,039
Total: $36,297

Out-of-State Tuition & Fees: $43,012 | **Additional Expenses:** $23,039
Total: $66,051

Financial Aid: https://www.financialaid.ucla.edu/

ADDITIONAL INFORMATION:

Available Degree(s)

- BA Theater, emphasis: Design/Production

Freshman Portfolio Requirement

Applicants must do the following:

- Submit the Undergraduate Theater Supplemental Application (via Acceptd)
- Virtual interview may be required if applicant is selected for one. However, interviews are not required for admission
- Personal insight questions
- Resume(s)
- Photograph
- Area of Interest Materials
  - Design Approach (2-page essay with a 2-4-page optional component of supporting images)
  - Portfolio (12 page PDF containing produced projects, costumes, scenery, props, scenic drafting, light plots, etc.)
- Unofficial transcript

For more information, visit: https://www.tft.ucla.edu/programs/theater-department/undergraduate-degrees/undergraduate-theater-program-ba/

Scholarships Offered

Theatre students at UCLA are eligible for numerous institutional, school wide, and departmental scholarships. For more information, visit: http://www.tft.ucla.edu/scholarships-2/

Special Opportunities

Students in the design/production emphasis may develop and produce a design in one of four areas: scenic, lighting, sound, costume.

Notable Alumni

- Kristin Hanggi: Broadway Director (*Rock of Ages*)
- John Rando: Broadway Director (*On the Town*)
- Hoyt Yeatman: Visual Effects Artist and Co-Founder of Dream Quest Images

UNIVERSITY OF SOUTHERN CALIFORNIA (USC)

Address: 1029 Childs Way, Los Angeles, CA 90089
Website: https://dramaticarts.usc.edu/
Contact: https://dramaticarts.usc.edu/contact/
Request for Information: https://uscsda.formstack.com/forms/checkinprospectonline
Phone: (213) 821-2744
Email: sdainfo@usc.edu

COST OF ATTENDANCE:

Tuition & Fees: $57,256 | **Additional Expenses:** $19,264
Total: $76,520

Financial Aid: https://financialaid.usc.edu/undergraduates/students.html

ADDITIONAL INFORMATION:

Available Degree(s)
- BFA Design
- BFA Sound Design
- BFA Stage Management
- BFA Technical Direction

Freshman Portfolio Requirement
- Submit via SlideRoom
- Headshot, resume, and essay response
- "Take Three" – 3 images that give insight into who you are
- Letter of recommendation from drama teacher
- 15 slides maximum of work you've completed in relation to the program
- Self-intro video (1-2 minutes maximum)
- Virtual portfolio review required, where applicant has conversation with production faculty and discusses their portfolio

For more information, visit: https://dramaticarts.usc.edu/programs/undergraduate/apply/bfa/

Scholarships Offered
The School of Dramatic Arts provides faculty-nominated merit-based awards to students who have completed at least one year as a Dramatic Arts major at USC. Among many, the Paul Allen Backer ISP Award is for "a student who shows exemplary talent in the creation and production of new plays and musicals within the Independent Student Production community". For more information, visit: https://dramaticarts.usc.edu/programs/undergraduate/tuition/

Special Opportunities
Located in Los Angeles, The USC School of Dramatic Arts allows students to study at a major center of American theatre. Through the Career Mentoring Program, senior-level student mentees can be matched with alumni mentors based on professional field interests and backgrounds.

Notable Alumni
- Vanessa J. Noon: Stage Manager and Production Manager for the Academy Awards; Stage Manager at Universal Studios Hollywood and Disneyland Resort
- Austin Wang: Director of the Taipei Performing Arts Center; Scenic and Lighting Designer
- Jeremy Pivnick: off-Broadway Lighting Designer; Senior Show Lighting Designer for Walt Disney Imagineering in Orlando

ALASKA

ARIZONA

CALIFORNIA

COLORADO

HAWAII

IDAHO

MONTANA

NEVADA

NEW MEXICO

OREGON

UTAH

WASHINGTON

WYOMING

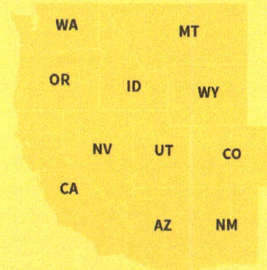

WEST

ALASKA

ARIZONA

CALIFORNIA

COLORADO

HAWAII

IDAHO

MONTANA

NEVADA

NEW MEXICO

OREGON

UTAH

WASHINGTON

WYOMING

UNIVERSITY OF NEVADA, LAS VEGAS (UNLV)

Address: 4505 S Maryland Pkwy, Las Vegas, NV 89154
Website: https://www.unlv.edu/degree/ba-theatre
Contact: https://www.unlv.edu/directories/contact
Request for Information: https://www.unlv.edu/learn-online/request-info
Phone: (702) 895-5390
Email: CFAAdvising@unlv.edu

COST OF ATTENDANCE:

In-State Tuition & Fees: $8,893 | **Additional Expenses:** $17,678
Total: $26,571

Out-of-State Tuition & Fees: $24,984 | **Additional Expenses:** $18,887
Total: $43,871

Financial Aid: https://www.unlv.edu/finaid

ADDITIONAL INFORMATION:

Available Degree(s)

- BA Theatre, concentration: Design/Technology

Freshman Portfolio Requirement

There is no portfolio requirement.

Scholarships Offered

Applicants are automatically considered for scholarships based on admission to the university and the completion of a Free Application for Federal Student Aid (FAFSA). The UNLV Western Undergraduate Exchange (WUE) scholarship is open to residents of a list of states and awards the difference between in-state and out-of-state tuition. For more information, visit: https://www.unlv.edu/finaid/scholarships-grants

The Department of Theatre awards approximately $20-$25,000 in undergraduate scholarships and grant-in-aid funds each academic year. Traditionally, students receive $1,000 to $2,500 annually. For more information, visit: https://www.unlv.edu/theatre/scholarships

Special Opportunities

UNLV also offers more engineering-based entertainment programs such as the BS in Entertainment Technology & Design and the BS in Entertainment Engineering and Design. For more information, visit: https://www.unlv.edu/degree/bs-entertainment-engineering-design

Notable Alumni

- Kevin Brekke: winner of American Ninja Warrior Obstacle Design Challenge
- Giovanna Sardelli: Director of New Works for TheatreWorks Silicon Valley

CORNISH COLLEGE OF THE ARTS (CALARTS)

Address: 1000 Lenora St, Seattle, WA 98121
Website: https://www.cornish.edu/cornish-programs/performance-production/
Contact: https://www.cornish.edu/contact/
Request for Information: N/A
Phone: (206) 726-2787
Email: hello@cornish.edu

COST OF ATTENDANCE:

Tuition & Fees: $40,464 | **Additional Expenses:** $16,080
Total: $56,544

Financial Aid: https://www.cornish.edu/tuition-financial-aid/

ADDITIONAL INFORMATION:

Available Degree(s)
- BFA Performance Production, concentrations:
  o Costume Design
  o Lighting Design
  o Scenic Design
  o Sound Design
  o Stage Management

Freshman Portfolio Requirement
- Costume Design
  o Pattern work, design drawings, street clothing, etc.
- Lighting Design
  o Lighting work examples, light plots, paperwork, instrument schedules, and any lighting-related experience in the form of photos, writing, and drafting
- Scenic Design
  o Any work in designing scenery for productions and that showcases applicant's understanding of 3D space
- Sound Design
  o Work that showcases experience with sound equipment, such as home stereo hook-ups or production-related sound
  o If applicant plays music, please include a sample
- Stage Management
  o Prompt books from productions applicant has worked, photos of productions, calendars, checklists, sign-up sheets, and other organizational evidence

For more information, visit: https://www.cornish.edu/audition-and-portfolio-main/performance-production-portfolio-requirements/

Scholarships Offered
Cornish merit scholarships are based on students' application and audition/portfolio review. No separate application is required for scholarship consideration. For more information, visit: http://www.cornish.edu/tuition-financial-aid/scholarships/

Special Opportunities
Students have access to three theatres, two scene shops, a costume shop, a metal shop, a woodshop, and a prop shop.

Notable Alumni
- Colleen Atwood: winner of Academy Award for Best Costume Design (*Memoirs of a Geisha, Alice in Wonderland,* and *Fantastic Beasts and Where to Find Them*)

ALASKA

ARIZONA

CALIFORNIA

COLORADO

HAWAII

IDAHO

MONTANA

NEVADA

NEW MEXICO

OREGON

UTAH

WASHINGTON

WYOMING

WEST

ALASKA

ARIZONA

CALIFORNIA

COLORADO

HAWAII

IDAHO

MONTANA

NEVADA

NEW MEXICO

OREGON

UTAH

WASHINGTON

WYOMING

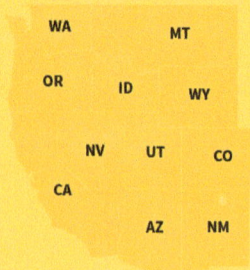

GONZAGA UNIVERSITY

Address: 502 E Boone Ave, Spokane, WA 99258
Website: https://www.gonzaga.edu/college-of-arts-sciences/
departments/theatre-dance/theatre
Contact: https://www.gonzaga.edu/contact-us
Request for Information: https://www.gonzaga.edu/
undergraduate-admission/contact/request-info
Phone: (509) 328-4220
Email: admissions@gonzaga.edu

COST OF ATTENDANCE:

Tuition & Fees: $48,470 | **Additional Expenses:** $18,191
Total: $66,661

Financial Aid: https://www.gonzaga.edu/admission/tuition-
scholarships-aid

ADDITIONAL INFORMATION:

Available Degree(s)

- BA Theatre Arts, concentration: Design, Technology, &
  Management

Freshman Portfolio Requirement

There is no portfolio. Interviews are optional.

Scholarships Offered

All applicants to Gonzaga University are automatically considered
for test-optional merit scholarships. The Act Six Scholarship
awards full-tuition or full-need scholarships to emerging urban and
community leaders from Tacoma, Seattle, or Spokane areas. For
more information, visit: https://www.gonzaga.edu/undergraduate-
admission/tuition-aid/scholarship-opportunities

Special Opportunities

The Theatre & Dance Department offers a minor in Interdisciplinary
Arts, which "expands a student's problem solving, critical reflection
and innovative thinking through combining the strengths of theatre,
dance, visual arts, and music." For more information, visit: https://
www.gonzaga.edu/college-of-arts-sciences/departments/theatre-
dance/interdisciplinary-arts

Theatre students may take advantage of study abroad and
internship opportunities in France, England, and Ireland. For
more information, visit: https://studyabroad.gonzaga.edu/index.
cfm?FuseAction=Programs.AdvancedSearch

CHAPTER 17

COSTUME DESIGN & TECHNICAL THEATRE SCHOOLS ALPHABETIZED BY CITY/STATE

School	City	State
Auburn University	Auburn	Alabama
University of Arizona	Tucson	Arizona
Loyola Marymount University (LMU)	Los Angeles	California
Otis College of Art and Design	Los Angeles	California
University of California, Los Angeles (UCLA)	Los Angeles	California
University of Southern California (USC)	Los Angeles	California
Pepperdine University	Malibu	California
Academy of Art University	San Francisco	California
California Institute of the Arts (CalArts)	Valencia	California
University of Connecticut	Storrs	Connecticut
Savannah College of Art and Design (SCAD)	Savannah	Georgia
University of Illinois Urbana-Champaign (UIUC)	Champaign	Illinois
Columbia College Chicago	Chicago	Illinois
DePaul University	Chicago	Illinois
Northwestern University	Evanston	Illinois
Indiana University at Bloomington	Bloomington	Indiana
University of Evansville	Evansville	Indiana
Ball State University	Muncie	Indiana
Purdue University	West Lafayette	Indiana
Wichita State University	Wichita	Kansas
Tulane University	New Orleans	Louisiana
Boston University	Boston	Massachusetts
Emerson College	Boston	Massachusetts
University of Michigan	Ann Arbor	Michigan
University of Missouri	Columbia	Missouri
Missouri State University	Springfield	Missouri
University of Nevada, Las Vegas (UNLV)	Las Vegas	Nevada
Montclair State University	Montclair	New Jersey
Rutgers University	New Brunswick	New Jersey
SUNY Binghamton	Binghamton	New York
CUNY NYC College of Technology	Brooklyn	New York
University at Buffalo	Buffalo	New York
Ithaca College	Ithaca	New York
Marymount Manhattan College	New York	New York
Pace University	New York	New York
SUNY Purchase	Purchase	New York

School	City	State
Skidmore College	Saratoga Springs	New York
Syracuse University	Syracuse	New York
Elon University	Elon	North Carolina
Catawba College	Salisbury	North Carolina
University of North Carolina School of the Arts	Winston-Salem	North Carolina
Baldwin Wallace University	Berea	Ohio
University of Cincinnati	Cincinnati	Ohio
Kent State University	Kent	Ohio
University of Oklahoma	Norman	Oklahoma
Oklahoma City University	Oklahoma City	Oklahoma
University of the Arts (UArts)	Philadelphia	Pennsylvania
Carnegie Mellon University	Pittsburgh	Pennsylvania
Pennsylvania State University	University Park	Pennsylvania
Belmont University	Nashville	Tennessee
Texas Christian University (TCU)	Fort Worth	Texas
Baylor University	Waco	Texas
Virginia Commonwealth University (VCU)	Richmond	Virginia
Shenandoah University	Winchester	Virginia
Cornish College of the Arts	Seattle	Washington
Gonzaga University	Spokane	Washington
University of Wisconsin	Madison	Wisconsin

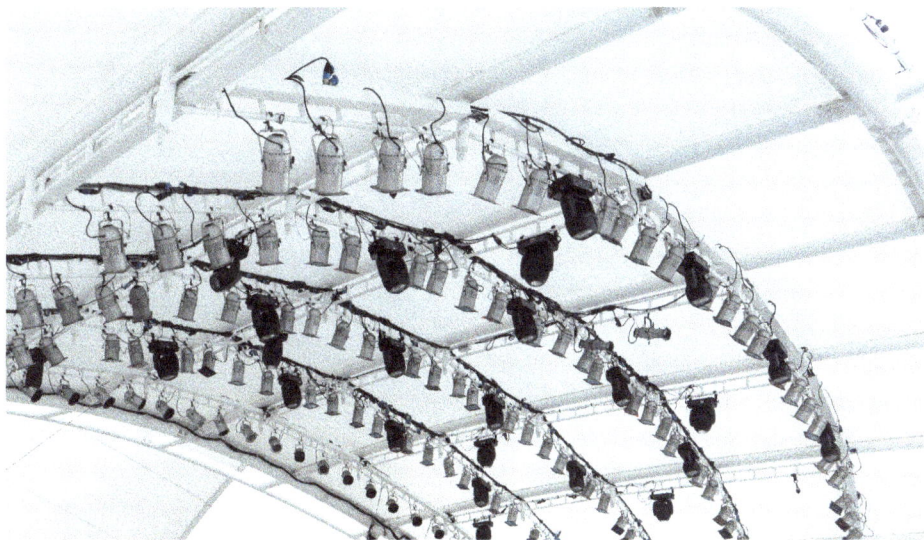

CHAPTER 18

TOP 10 SCHOOLS FOR COSTUME DESIGN

*Note: NYU and Yale only offer graduate programs in Costume Design. Thus, they are not listed in this book. Additionally, while University of the Arts, London is an excellent school, it is located outside of the United States and is therefore not listed in the profiles in this book.

Ranking	School
1	California Institute of the Arts (CalArts)
2	Carnegie Mellon University
3	New York University (NYU)
4	Savannah College of Art & Design (SCAD)
5	University of California, Los Angeles (UCLA)
6	University of Missouri-Kansas City
7	University of the Arts, London (UAL)
8	University of North Carolina School of the Arts (UNCSA)
9	University of Southern California
10	Yale School of Drama

Source: https://www.hollywoodreporter.com/lists/the-worlds-top-10-costume-design-schools/usc-school-of-dramatic-arts-8/#

CHAPTER 19

TOP 10 SCHOOLS FOR TECHNICAL THEATRE

Ranking	School
1	University of North Carolina School of the Arts (UNCSA)
2	California Institute of the Arts (CalArts)
3	SUNY Purchase
4	Savannah College of Art & Design (SCAD)
5	University of Cincinnati
6	University of Arizona
7	Boston University
8	Cornish College of the Arts
9	DePaul University
10	Emerson College

Source: https://www.collegeraptor.com/Majors/Details/50.0502/Level/Bachelors-degree/State/All/Technical-Theatre-Theatre-Design-and-Technology/

CHAPTER 20

COSTUME DESIGN & TECHNICAL THEATRE SCHOOLS BY AVERAGE TEST SCORE

COSTUME DESIGN & TECHNICAL THEATRE SCHOOLS BY AVERAGE SAT SCORE

School	Avg. SAT
Catawba College	470-570 (ERW)
	470-570 (M)
Montclair State University	490-590 (ERW)
	490-570 (M)
	*Test optional
Marymount Manhattan College	500-580 (ERW)
	460-620 (M)
Kent State University	510-610 (ERW)
	510-600 (M)
Missouri State University	510-610 (ERW)
	510-610 (M)
Wichita State University	510-620 (ERW)
	510-630 (M)
Shenandoah University	510-630 (ERW)
	500-600 (M)
University of Nevada, Las Vegas (UNLV)	520-620 (ERW)
	510-630 (M)
Baldwin Wallace University	520-640 (ERW)
	520-620 (M)
DePaul University	530-640 (ERW)
	530-640 (M)
Pennsylvania State University	530-640 (ERW)
	540-660 (M)
Pace University	540-630 (ERW)
	520-610 (M)
Savannah College of Art and Design (SCAD)	540-640 (ERW)
	500-600 (M)
Virginia Commonwealth University (VCU)	540-640 (ERW)
	520-610 (M)
Oklahoma City University	550-650 (ERW)
	530-610 (M)
University of Arizona	550-660 (ERW)
	540-690 (M)

218

School	Avg. SAT
University at Buffalo	560-640 (ERW)
	580-670 (M)
University of Oklahoma	560-650 (ERW)
	540-650 (M)
University of Cincinnati	560-650 (ERW)
	560-680 (M)
SUNY Purchase	560-660 (ERW)
	540-620 (M)
Texas Christian University (TCU)	560-660 (ERW)
	550-660 (M)
University of Missouri	560-660 (ERW)
	550-660 (M)
Indiana University at Bloomington	560-670 (ERW)
	560-680 (M)
Belmont University	580-660 (ERW)
	540-640 (M)
Elon University	580-660 (ERW)
	560-660 (M)
Gonzaga University	580-670 (ERW)
	580-680 (M)
Syracuse University	580-670 (ERW)
	600-710 (M)
University of Connecticut	580-680 (ERW)
	590-710 (M)
Purdue University	580-680 (ERW)
	590-740 (M)
Rutgers University	580-680 (ERW)
	600-730 (M)
Auburn University	590-650 (ERW)
	570-670 (M)
University of North Carolina School of the Arts	590-670 (ERW)
	530-640 (M)
Ithaca College	590-670 (ERW)
	570-650 (M)

School	Avg. SAT
University of Illinois Urbana-Champaign (UIUC)	590-690 (ERW) 610-770 (M)
Baylor University	600-680 (ERW) 590-680 (M)
Pepperdine University	600-690 (ERW) 600-720 (M)
Emerson College	610-690 (ERW) 580-690 (M)
Loyola Marymount University (LMU)	610-690 (ERW) 600-700 (M)
University of Wisconsin	610-690 (ERW) 650-770 (M)
Skidmore College	610-700 (ERW) 610-700 (M)
SUNY Binghamton	640-710 (ERW) 650-740 (M)
Boston University	640-720 (ERW) 670-780 (M)
University of California, Los Angeles (UCLA)	640-740 (ERW) 640-790 (M)
Tulane University	650-730 (ERW) 690-770 (M)
University of Michigan	660-740 (ERW) 680-780 (M)
University of Southern California (USC)	660-740 (ERW) 680-790 (M)
Northwestern University	700-760 (ERW) 730-790 (M)
Carnegie Mellon University	700-760 (ERW) 760-800 (M)
CUNY NYC College of Technology	N/A
California Institute of the Arts (CalArts)	N/A *Test optional

220

School	Avg. SAT
Columbia College Chicago	N/A *Test optional
Cornish College of the Arts	N/A *Test optional
Academy of Art University	N/A *Open admissions
Ball State University	N/A *Test optional
Otis College of Art and Design	N/A *Test optional
University of Evansville	N/A *Test optional
University of the Arts (UArts)	N/A *Test optional

COSTUME DESIGN & TECHNICAL THEATRE SCHOOLS BY AVERAGE ACT SCORE

School	Avg. ACT
Catawba College	17-22 (ACT C)
University of Nevada, Las Vegas (UNLV)	19-25 (ACT C)
Shenandoah University	19-26 (ACT C)
Kent State University	20-26 (ACT C)
Savannah College of Art and Design (SCAD)	20-27 (ACT C)
Wichita State University	20-27 (ACT C)
Marymount Manhattan College	20-28 (ACT C)
Baldwin Wallace University	21-27 (ACT C)
Missouri State University	21-27 (ACT C)
Virginia Commonwealth University (VCU)	21-28 (ACT C)
University of Arizona	21-29 (ACT C)
Pace University	22-28 (ACT C)
Oklahoma City University	22-29 (ACT C)
University of North Carolina School of the Arts	22-29 (ACT C)
University at Buffalo	23-29 (ACT C)
University of Cincinnati	23-29 (ACT C)
University of Missouri	23-29 (ACT C)
University of Oklahoma	23-29 (ACT C)
Belmont University	23-30 (ACT C)
Pennsylvania State University	24-29 (ACT C)
SUNY Purchase	24-30 (ACT C)
Indiana University at Bloomington	24-31 (ACT C)
Elon University	25-30 (ACT C)
Gonzaga University	25-30 (ACT C)
Auburn University	25-31 (ACT C)
Texas Christian University (TCU)	25-31 (ACT C)
Rutgers University	25-32 (ACT C)
Purdue University	25-33 (ACT C)
Syracuse University	26-30 (ACT C)
Baylor University	26-31 (ACT C)
Ithaca College	26-31 (ACT C)
Pepperdine University	26-31 (ACT C)
Emerson College	27-31 (ACT C)
Loyola Marymount University (LMU)	27-31 (ACT C)

School	Avg. ACT
Skidmore College	27-31(ACT C)
University of Connecticut	27-32 (ACT C)
University of Wisconsin	27-32 (ACT C)
University of Illinois Urbana-Champaign (UIUC)	27-33 (ACT C)
University of California, Los Angeles (UCLA)	27-34 (ACT C)
SUNY Binghamton	29-32 (ACT C)
Tulane University	30-33 (ACT C)
University of Southern California (USC)	30-34 (ACT C)
Boston University	30-34 (ACT C)
University of Michigan	31-34 (ACT C)
Carnegie Mellon University	33-35 (ACT C)
Northwestern University	33-35 (ACT)
CUNY NYC College of Technology	N/A
DePaul University	N/A
Academy of Art University	N/A *Open admissions
California Institute of the Arts (CalArts)	N/A *Test optional
Columbia College Chicago	N/A *Test optional
Cornish College of the Arts	N/A *Test optional
Ball State University	N/A *Test optional
Montclair State University	N/A *Test optional
Otis College of Art and Design	N/A *Test optional
University of Evansville	N/A *Test optional
University of the Arts (UArts)	N/A *Test optional

COSTUME DESIGN & TECHNICAL THEATRE SCHOOLS BY AVERAGE GPA

School	Avg. GPA
Otis College of Art and Design	3.26
Montclair State University	3.3
SUNY Purchase	3.33
University of Arizona	3.43
University of Nevada, Las Vegas (UNLV)	3.43
Emerson College	3.5
Wichita State University	3.51
Ball State University	3.52
Shenandoah University	3.55
Tulane University	3.55
Catawba College	3.59
Savannah College of Art and Design (SCAD)	3.6
Kent State University	3.61
University of Oklahoma	3.63
Baldwin Wallace University	3.64
Purdue University	3.67
Syracuse University	3.67
Gonzaga University	3.69
Pepperdine University	3.69
University of North Carolina School of the Arts	3.69
University at Buffalo	3.7
University of Cincinnati	3.7
Virginia Commonwealth University (VCU)	3.72
Missouri State University	3.73
Indiana University at Bloomington	3.75
Boston University	3.76
DePaul University	3.8
Belmont University	3.83
University of Southern California (USC)	3.83
Carnegie Mellon University	3.85
Loyola Marymount University (LMU)	3.85
University of Michigan	3.87
University of Wisconsin	3.87
University of California, Los Angeles (UCLA)	3.9

School	Avg. GPA
Auburn University	3.97
Elon University	4.04
Baylor University	N/A
California Institute of the Arts (CalArts)	N/A
Columbia College Chicago	N/A
Cornish College of the Arts	N/A
CUNY NYC College of Technology	N/A
Ithaca College	N/A
Marymount Manhattan College	N/A
Northwestern University	N/A
Oklahoma City University	N/A
Pace University	N/A
Pennsylvania State University	N/A
Rutgers University	N/A
Skidmore College	N/A
SUNY Binghamton	N/A
Texas Christian University (TCU)	N/A
University of Connecticut	N/A
University of Evansville	N/A
University of Illinois Urbana-Champaign (UIUC)	N/A
University of Missouri	N/A
University of the Arts (UArts)	N/A
Academy of Art University	N/A *Open admissions

JOURNEY TO ART, DANCE, MUSIC, THEATRE, FILM, AND FASHION SERIES

JOURNEY TO
Fashion Design
COLLEGE ADMISSIONS & PROFILES

RACHEL A. WINSTON, PH.D.

JOURNEY TO
Fashion Merchandising
COLLEGE ADMISSIONS & PROFILES

RACHEL A. WINSTON, PH.D.

JOURNEY TO
Costume Design & Technical Theatre
COLLEGE ADMISSIONS & PROFILES

RACHEL A. WINSTON, PH.D.

JOURNEY TO
Theatre and the Dramatic Arts
COLLEGE ADMISSIONS & PROFILES

RACHEL A. WINSTON, PH.D.

JOURNEY TO
Musical
Theatre
COLLEGE ADMISSIONS & PROFILES

RACHEL A. WINSTON, PH.D.

Live your dreams today remembering that discipline is the bridge between dreams and achievement!

"We believe in the American Dream that all people rich or poor can go as far in life as their talents and persistence will take them."
– Lizard Publishing Vision

At Lizard, we help you make your dreams come true.

CONTACT INFORMATION

Phone: 949-833-7706
E-mail: collegeguide@yahoo.com
Website: collegelizard.com and Lizard-publishing.com

228

COMPREHENSIVE HEALTH CARE SERIES

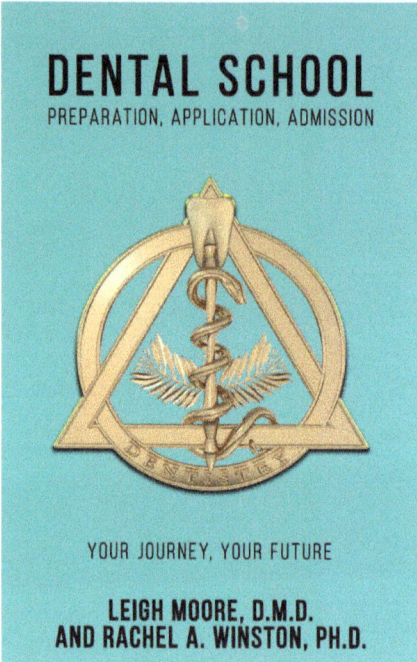

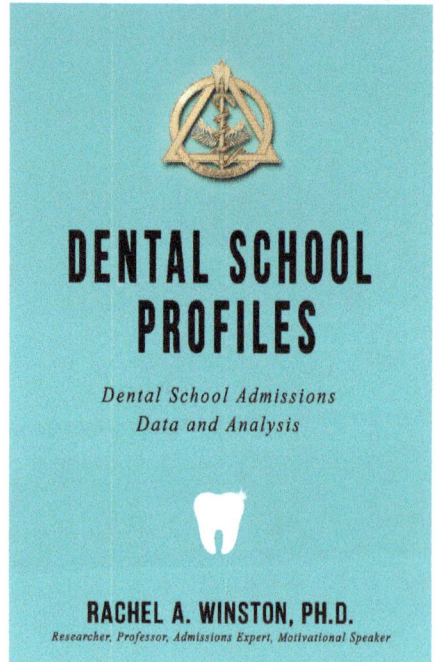

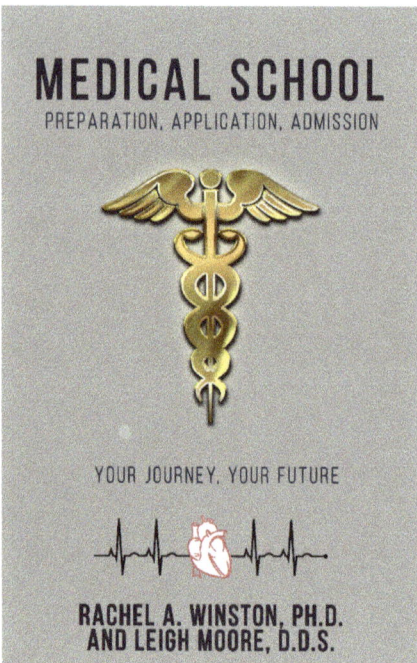

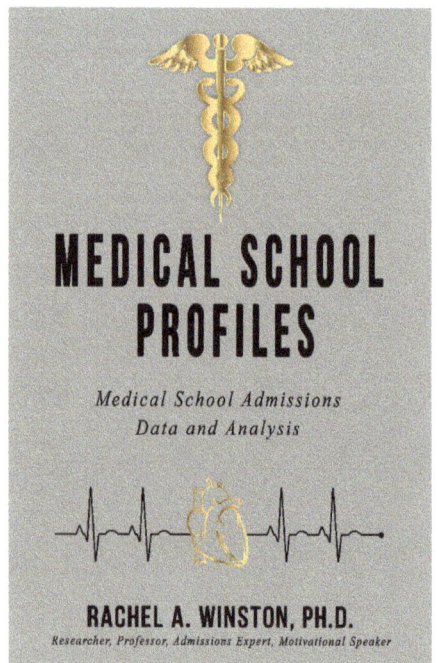

DENTAL SCHOOL

PREPARATION, APPLICATION, ADMISSION

YOUR JOURNEY, YOUR FUTURE

LEIGH MOORE, D.M.D.
AND RACHEL A. WINSTON, PH.D.

DENTAL SCHOOL PROFILES

Dental School Admissions Data and Analysis

RACHEL A. WINSTON, PH.D.
Researcher, Professor, Admissions Expert, Motivational Speaker

MEDICAL SCHOOL

PREPARATION, APPLICATION, ADMISSION

YOUR JOURNEY, YOUR FUTURE

RACHEL A. WINSTON, PH.D.
AND LEIGH MOORE, D.D.S.

MEDICAL SCHOOL PROFILES

Medical School Admissions Data and Analysis

RACHEL A. WINSTON, PH.D.
Researcher, Professor, Admissions Expert, Motivational Speaker

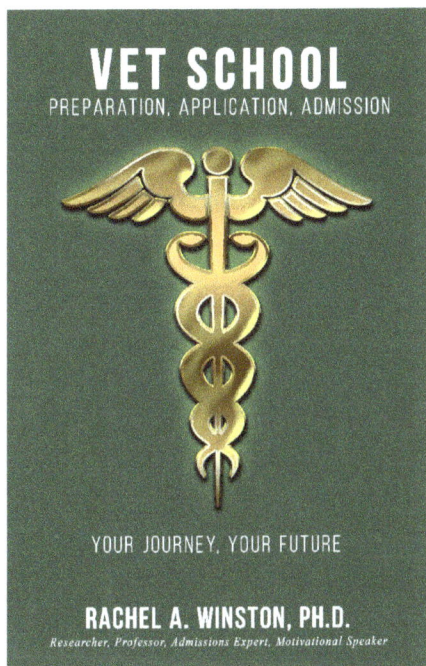

VET SCHOOL
PREPARATION, APPLICATION, ADMISSION

YOUR JOURNEY, YOUR FUTURE

RACHEL A. WINSTON, PH.D.
Researcher, Professor, Admissions Expert, Motivational Speaker

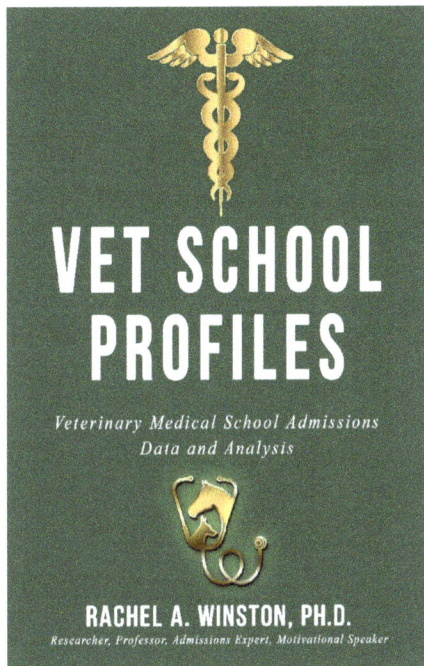

VET SCHOOL PROFILES

Veterinary Medical School Admissions Data and Analysis

RACHEL A. WINSTON, PH.D.
Researcher, Professor, Admissions Expert, Motivational Speaker

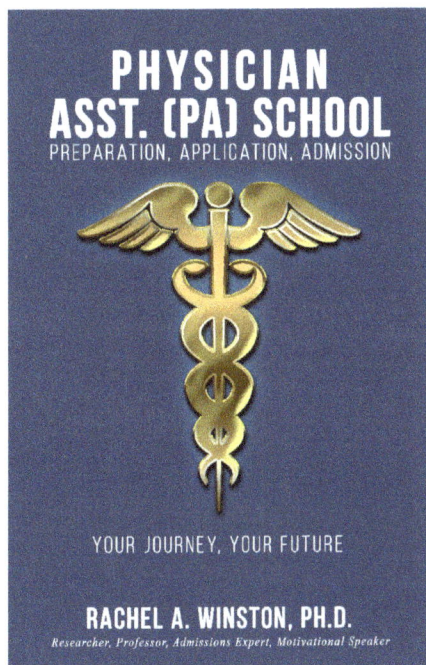

PHYSICIAN ASST. (PA) SCHOOL
PREPARATION, APPLICATION, ADMISSION

YOUR JOURNEY, YOUR FUTURE

RACHEL A. WINSTON, PH.D.
Researcher, Professor, Admissions Expert, Motivational Speaker

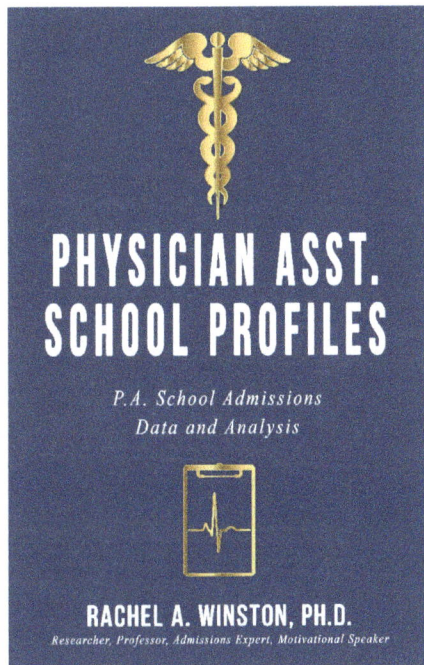

PHYSICIAN ASST. SCHOOL PROFILES

P.A. School Admissions Data and Analysis

RACHEL A. WINSTON, PH.D.
Researcher, Professor, Admissions Expert, Motivational Speaker

PHARM.D. SCHOOL
PREPARATION, APPLICATION, ADMISSION

YOUR JOURNEY, YOUR FUTURE

RACHEL A. WINSTON, PH.D.
Researcher, Professor, Admissions Expert, Motivational Speaker

PHARM.D. SCHOOL PROFILES

Pharmacy School Admissions Data and Analysis

RACHEL A. WINSTON, PH.D.
Researcher, Professor, Admissions Expert, Motivational Speaker

OSTEOPATHIC MEDICAL SCHOOL
PREPARATION, APPLICATION, ADMISSION

YOUR JOURNEY, YOUR FUTURE

RACHEL A. WINSTON, PH.D.
Researcher, Professor, Admissions Expert, Motivational Speaker

OSTEO SCHOOL PROFILES

Osteopathic Medical School Admissions Data and Analysis

RACHEL A. WINSTON, PH.D.
Researcher, Professor, Admissions Expert, Motivational Speaker

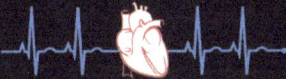

This comprehensive healthcare series is designed in full color to aid the growing number of applicants seeking clear, comprehensive materials. As a college admissions expert and former UCLA College Counseling Certificate Program faculty member, Dr. Winston is dedicated to helping students obtain the information they need.

FOR MORE INFORMATION

bsmdguide.com

medschoolexpert.com

Purchase books at Lizard-publishing.com

SERVICES OFFERED BY LIZARD EDUCATION:

- College Counseling
- Admissions News/Resources
- Essay Support and Editing
- Interview Preparation
- Road Trips to Visit Colleges
- Career Planning/Majors/ Resumes
- BS/MD, BS/DO, BS/JD, BS/DDS
- Medical School
- Graduate School (Masters & Doctorate)

- Film Studio and Editing
- Portfolio Assistance/SlideRoom
- Athletics Recruiting/Highlight Films
- International Admissions/Visa/ TOEFL
- Financial Aid and Scholarships
- UCs, Ivy Leagues, and Colleges Nationwide
- Book Publishing
- Engineering, Robotics, STEM
- Art Portfolios

Email: collegeguide@yahoo.com

Website: collegelizard.com

LIZARD

INDEX

A

D

E

N

O

P

T

U

V

W

Y

Z

www.ingramcontent.com/pod-product-compliance
Lightning Source LLC
Chambersburg PA
CBHW041936260326
41914CB00010B/1318